JOURNEY INTO FREEDOM

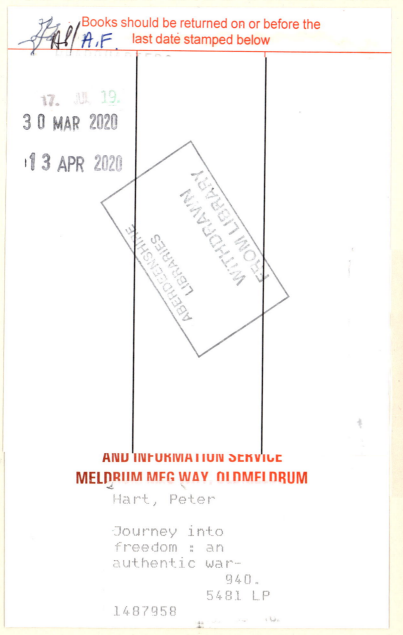

JOURNEY INTO FREEDOM

An Authentic War-Time Story

Peter Hart

ISIS
LARGE PRINT
Oxford

First published in Great Britain 2003
by Authors OnLine Ltd.

Published in Large Print 2003 by ISIS Publishing Ltd,
7 Centremead, Osney Mead, Oxford OX2 0ES
by arrangement with Peter Hart

The moral right of the author has been asserted

British Library Cataloguing in Publication Data
Hart, Peter
Journey into freedom: an authentic war-time story.
– Large print ed. – (Isis reminiscence series)
1. Hart, Peter
2. World War, 1939–1945 – Personal narratives,
British 3. Intelligence officers – Great Britain –
Biography 4. Large type books
I. Title
940.5'48141

ISBN 0–7531–9926–2 (hb)
ISBN 0–7531–9927–0 (pb)

Printed and bound by Antony Rowe, Chippenham

Contents

Foreword

This book is a dedication to my friends and acquaintances, who through no fault of their own were persecuted during the Second World War in Europe.

I remember many of the brave people putting their own lives at risk, by offering sanctuary and help to the thousands of refugees and prisoners of war, trying to escape the common enemy.

Yet I recall some of the happier times during those dark days and the courage of all my friends in adversity.

I also dedicate this book to my late father, mother and sister as well as Dr. Bell, former Bishop of Chichester, and to all my friends mentioned in it without whose unstinted support and help I would not have been able to complete my journey.

I would also like to thank my daughter Monica and her husband Paul for all the help they have given me with the preparation of this book.

Finally, my thanks go to my wife Lili for her constant help, encouragement and patience while writing this book and for editing it.

CHAPTER
ONE

Nobody paid attention to the very French-looking young man of 28, who boarded the train at Montauban on the 12th November 1942 with a false French identity card, provided some time earlier by a friend of old standing.

A few days before, the Germans had occupied the so-called "FreeZone" of France, following the Allied landing in North Africa on November 8th.

As the Vichy authorities had been assiduously rounding up foreigners, especially Jews, for months before, in anticipation of the arrival of the Germans, I had been living in hiding for some time, determined to make my way to England, come what may.

This, then, was the first part of my long "Journey into Freedom".

It was only when we were approaching Narbonne, just north of Perpignan, near the border with Spain that the whole folly of my adventure struck me.

My immediate aim was to reach Bourg-Madame, a small village on the French side of the frontier with Spain, where I had been given the address of a Spanish gourd-maker, those leather wine bottles from which the

Spaniards can so deftly squeeze wine into their throats from a considerable distance.

I had not yet spoken to any of my companions in the compartment. Two of them were obviously sisters who had joined the train at Toulouse. As I was soon to find out, they were Spanish and on their way from their home in Zaragossa to Lyons in France, where the younger one of the two was to be married to a Frenchman. My journey was, of course, of a less romantic nature, but as I was talking to them, the idea suddenly came to me that this chance encounter would provide me with a good reason for journeying towards the Spanish border, which was essential now that the Germans were in position there. What better excuse than to play the role of the "fiancé" of the young Spanish lady, collecting her at the border!

This was my first train journey during the war when I was actually travelling with civilians and had paid my own fare.

I had to change trains at Perpignan and stop overnight. The Germans had already arrived before me and occupied all the rooms in the hotels.

I had no desire to be picked up in the streets by one of their patrols, so there was only one place to make for, the local whorehouse or bordel, as it is called in France.

I was hardly in the mood to make full use of their facilities, but I was able to strike a bargain and got what may be called "a room without", where I could get some sleep until my train for Bourg-Madame left early the next morning.

I had scarcely sat down, when a gendarme on the train came through, asking for identity papers and I was frantically re-thinking the story I had prepared, should he ask me why I was going to the Spanish border.

I had obtained the names of the two sisters, my travel companions of the previous day, having decided that the reason for my going up to the border was to welcome them as the "fiancé", whom one of them was actually meeting in Lyons at that moment. It would not matter, I explained to myself, working the whole thing out in detail, that my "fiancée" could not be there in person, since she was by now already in Lyons, but it would give me a good reason for spending the night in Bourg-Madame, so that I would be able to organise my escape without arousing suspicion.

However, no use putting the cart before the horse. Just now the gendarme was getting nearer and nearer to where I was sitting. I took out my false identity card, the photograph was well fixed, they had made a good job of it, and I knew that my French would stand up to being questioned. Nevertheless, my heart was thumping as I did not fancy being questioned so near to my goal and being handed over to the Germans.

How does one behave in these situations? Look the gendarme straight in the eyes, make a joke, ignore him and speak to a fellow passenger, casually waving the identity card towards him? Or does one make a dash for the loo, or perhaps pretend to have known him as a friend for donkey's years, waving to him in a familiar manner, hoping that he is then embarrassed to have forgotten your name and face?

In the end I meekly tendered my card to him the way you would present your ticket to a ticket-inspector and luckily that worked without any questions asked; so I never found out about the alternatives!

When we got to Bourg-Madame I made straight for my gourd-maker who had his boutique at the end of the village. I was fortunate in finding him alone, as I did not carry any letters of introduction which would have been rather foolish under the circumstances. I hoped that I had been announced by my Quaker friends back in Montauban and would be greeted as a friend and be complimented at having made it so far! In fact, the gourd-maker barely looked up from his work.

"A guide now, with the Germans swarming all over, quite impossible", he said. "You should have come a few days earlier!" I would not be put off so easily and I told him that I was sure a man so highly recommended, who had helped so many others, would not let me down because of a few Germans. I would now go to the hotel and expect him to arrange something and call on me later in the day. I heard him mumbling something in Spanish and went off to the local hotel, which on arrival I found swarming with German soldiers and French gendarmes. However, no-one seemed to bother with me, even when I settled down in the restaurant where I was the only civilian among all the uniforms!

I rehearsed the story about my fiancée coming from Spain, whom I was to meet at La Tour-de-Carol, the nearby railway frontier station, where I was quite sure she had not passed. I even took the precaution, just before lunch, to walk up to the gendarmes at the station and to enquire from them whether she had passed that day, identifying myself in their eyes as her fiancé, giving them the name of my false identity card, Jean-Pierre Blanvin, and asking them to please let me know at once at the hotel, should she come through. All this appeared to be unnecessary, because nobody questioned me as to why I was there, but attack is better than defence and after lunch I went to my room and fell fast asleep. I think it is only when you are young that you have such "sangfroid" — going to sleep in the middle of the day, under these circumstances — and I have often since wondered what I would have done had I been middle-aged; probably worried myself sick!

I had been asleep for a couple of hours or so, when a loud knock at the door woke me up. I must admit, I did get a bit of a shock, but somehow I knew it would be my Spaniard, although I was still drowsy when I opened the door. Sure enough, there he stood and he did not waste much time either. We spoke in French, my Spanish being non-existent at that time. As I gathered my wits together, a warm glow of anticipation came over me, surely he would not have come to see me, unless he was prepared to help me over the mountains.

I did not have to wait long. He wanted to know how much money I had. My reply that I had none did not seem to put him off and I offered him the golden fob belonging to the golden watch, both of which my father had given to me when I saw him for the very last time some eight years before. The fob had been given to him by some of his friends, whose names were engraved on it. It almost seemed to me as if he had foreseen such a situation for his son and I knew that he would not mind if I used it to pay my guide to freedom.

As for the watch, I kept it throughout the war — the only personal momento I possessed — and through it I met my wife Lili in 1944, as if my father who had died by then, was still looking after me. But that is a different story!

Back to my guide: to my great relief he was willing to accept the gold fob and now began to give me his instructions. There was to be no talk of how little I had contributed for the guide, as an exiled Spaniard was returning to Spain in the same party and he had paid a lot more. When arriving on the other side of the border I would be staying with the gourd-maker's family and under no circumstances must I leave the house, the guide would take me further inland the following day.

He told me to wait in the bar of the hotel at nine o'clock that night without any luggage or carrying anything at all and to follow him outside when I saw him using his handkerchief. I should then continue to follow him and when he passed a man with a glowing cigarette I would know that he was my guide and I should follow that fellow.

So that was it and he left, having assured me that at 9 o'clock at night it would be dark and the Germans were usually having their dinner and would be very thin on the ground; the chances were that nobody would spot our small party of three who were to make their border-crossing not over the mountains, but at ground level! What impudent confidence!

However, before I continue I must now mention how I reached this point and explain why "My Journey" was really necessary.

CHAPTER
TWO

Like most other people of my generation, I shall never forget the Sunday, early in September 1939, when it came over the loudspeaker that "a state of war" now existed, as no reply had been received from Berlin to the British ultimatum.

We were having lunch, my Director, his wife, a colleague and myself at the "Centre de Réclassement Professionnel" in Martigny-les-Bains (in the western part of the Vosges Department) not far from Burgundy, which had been founded earlier that year by Baron Robert de Rothschild, of the Paris branch of the family, for the professional retraining of refugees from Germany and Austria, who had left their countries to escape from the Nazis and had tried to make France their home.

Martigny used to be a busy Spa, and the "Hotel International" which had been rented to house the students and to provide workshops and lecture rooms, must have seen better days.

When the project was still in the planning stage, I had received an invitation from Baron Robert to call at his office in the Rue de Cirque "on a matter which may interest me". I had been working for the Rothschild

"Co-ordinating Committee for Help and Protection" for a little while already as a volunteer, having one day walked into the Rothschild Banking House in November 1938, offering my services. They were accepted and I was then working for Baron Guy de Rothschild, after he had taken up references with Major Frank Goldsmith, the hotel tycoon and father of Jimmy Goldsmith. Major Goldsmith had shown interest in my hotel career and was later instrumental in obtaining a post for me at the King David Hotel in Jerusalem, which I could not take up as war interfered. At that time I did not know Baron Robert, but one day early in December 1938, I happened to meet him on the stairs of the office and was introduced to him.

Later that month I was asked to call at no. 23 Avenue Marigny, where I was offered an administrative position, as assistant to the French Director to be, and I was asked if I would be willing to accept on a voluntary basis, meaning without a salary. I have always loved to start things from scratch, having worked in the hotel industry in France and Italy since 1933 when, anticipating the horrors of what was to come, I had left Germany at the age of 18. I therefore considered the Centre a great challenge and immediately accepted the offer, although I had meanwhile been granted a visa for Britain!

This had been obtained on the guarantee of a good friend of mine, Eric Benzinger, whose hospitality I had enjoyed in Paris when I arrived there in May 1933. Eric, the son of friends of my parents, was a most generous and warm-hearted person. He was married to a beautiful French girl, Raymonde, whom I only met much later in 1944 when she had become a widow, as Eric had, tragically, been killed in action. Although I had various connections in England, it was by no means certain that I would be allowed to work there and I finally decided, after consulting my parents, that Baron Rothschild's project should be given a chance and that I would be more useful at the Centre than in England. Little did I realize then that this decision would trap me in France at the outbreak of war, separate me from my family, make me a prisoner of the Germans and that it would take years to reach the UK in 1943 after so many tribulations and hardships!

The project of the Centre was well planned and provided re-training by experts in many fields of light industry and various crafts, even including a farm nearby. The students who had been in occupations and professions which offered them no hope of employment in France or in other countries to which they might eventually emigrate, were thus given an opportunity to obtain skills for jobs which would be more easily available to them than those they were qualified for before they became refugees.

So one cold winter's day at the end of February 1939, an advance party consisting of my Director to be, myself and a colleague, together with a cook and a handyman, arrived at the Hotel International. From the outside it looked very imposing. Indeed, one could imagine it in its former glory. However, nobody had prepared us for what we would find inside. The place had not been occupied since it had served as a camp for Spanish refugees during the Spanish Civil war. Its state defied description!

When we had a look at some of the rooms we thought that they could not possibly all be that bad, but they were. Wallpaper was hanging from the walls in strips and everything from the floor upwards was black with dirt; cobwebs hung everywhere. There were no washbasins in any of the bedrooms and no running water on any of the floors. It was icy cold and no stove in sight!

There was no time to waste if we wanted to sleep that night and get some rooms ready for the first arrivals in two days' time. We worked until we collapsed late that evening and for twenty hours the next day. When the first arrivals came, they simply had to re-enforce us to prepare the rooms for the time when training courses were to start. In the large dining room a vast amount of equipment was stored. It had arrived from Paris earlier on and consisted of beds, mattresses, blankets, kitchen and office equipment, machines, work benches, tools and various stores. Everything was brand-new and still wrapped up. The task of sorting it all out and distributing it demanded a lot of teamwork, which was from the beginning the key word for this type of operation, where all the work done was for the benefit of everybody. In fact, all students were assigned duties when they were not attending courses, so that the Centre could be run without outside help.

It was made clear to the students from the outset that the various jobs they were doing, whether it was in the kitchen, public rooms, workshops or lavatories were not "fatigues", but necessary routine maintenance for the smooth running of the Centre. Little did we know at the time that this training, in particular, would prove very beneficial in war-time.

When the courses finally started there were about 100 students and later on double that number, among them married couples, but no single girls, who apparently did not need any re-training.

Lecturers in the various subjects to be taught arrived and prepared the curriculum. We acquired a small farm near the hotel, about 70 acres. A blond ex-gym teacher from Vienna, Schindler, who already looked very much like a French farmer, was in charge of thirty students who had never worked the land before, but took to the work like ducks to water. There were five cows and two horses, forty hens and some cocks.

A vegetable garden was soon created which together with the milk and eggs, and later, butter and cheese, reduced the need for outside supplies. A special lecturer from an agricultural college was also engaged to teach the students about the cultivation of the soil. I was also in charge of supervising the produce of the farm and there I learnt my first lesson when I discovered, a little too late, that the number of hens always remained the same in their weekly reports, in spite of the cocks being present in the farmyard. Something was wrong, as the Centre had never received a chicken. On investigation I discovered that my good farmers had been gorging themselves with chicken! Every time a young chick was hatched, a grown chicken went into the pot! Well, I suppose they wanted to become self-sufficient.

12

The first arrival of a calf caused some excitement, but during the night the poor mother-cow felt queer and became quite ill, so I was woken up, had to get a vet and rush over to calm everybody down. I am glad to say that after some blood-letting the old girl continued to give us excellent milk and her calf became the mascot of our farm.

Meanwhile, in the main building, the courses had also started and the Centre looked like a University for all ages. The workshops buzzed with activity and a lot of noise could be heard. Teachers from Technical Colleges, re-inforced several times a week by Professors from nearby Epinal, hoped to produce good results within six months, due to intensive teaching and practical work, designed for short courses, on which nine hours a day were spent. The majority of students in spite of the long periods of idleness since their arrival in France had adapted well, although some had never worked before and others had no experience of manual labour.

In the metal workshop one would find ex-lawyers and commercial travellers working on the same bench, proud to show their workman-like hands. In the forge, installed in an annexe of the hotel, one encountered ex-students of philosophy and in the welding shop one could see still inexperienced students in their protective gear handle heavy bottles of oxygen, instead of dictionaries.

In the carpenters' shops, very elegant and clean in comparison to the other departments, bookshelves, tables and chairs were already produced. Shoe repairing was another important subject, especially as the students' shoes needed constant attention. One of the students proved to be such a fantastic story-teller that many a hammer remained suspended in mid-air.

The women, all married to a man in the centre, were not taught any technical subjects but received instructions in making new clothes and repairing old ones, as well as hat-making and fashion design.

An electrical workshop and a mechanical course for motorcar repairs were also on the drawing board.

I often wondered what the older students, who had been in professions, in industry and trade, made of all this. Did they think that this was really "not them", or did they genuinely believe they would be able to earn their living in the jobs they were being taught?

My own task at the Centre was, in the first instance, to assist the Director, M. Bouley, in his job of running the Centre. He was a typical French Civil Servant with previous experience in this field, but he did not speak a single word of German, so I had constantly to interpret. In addition, I had to fulfil the combined duties of many hotel staff, to which, through my previous experiences and training, I was already used. Reception and settling in of new arrivals, receiving supplies and dishing them out, supervising the kitchen, arranging the menu, paying the bills, keeping accounts, looking after maintenance and dealing with correspondence.

However, this was not all. As will be seen from what follows, human problems, either real or imagined had also to be dealt with every day of the week, including Sundays.

I was valiantly assisted in this task by a fellow refugee from Vienna, Fred Godel, with whom I got on extremely well, although our temperaments were very different. He was so easy-going, I always admired him for this, clever and lazy at the same time and with a good sense of humour. I took everything much more seriously and often wished I had his happy-go-lucky attitude.

Of course, with so many people under one roof — there were, by now, 200 — who had only one thing in common, namely that they were all refugees from Nazi oppression — there were always personal problems to solve and often disputes among students had to be settled, quite apart from organising the courses and the day-to-day running of the Centre.

There were also communal problems which were most likely brought about by wrong selection of candidates and too rosy a picture about the Centre being painted by the Selection Committee. The intention was to re-train refugees for manual jobs and the reason why this was not done in towns like Paris, was that the Centre had been created to give refuge for those whose permits to stay in France had expired and for those who had no homes, thus combining re-training with giving these refugees a roof over their heads, food and the permission to stay in France, as long as they stayed at the Centre.

Many of the students selected had lived in far better circumstances than the Centre could offer and felt they had given up a more comfortable existence in exchange for learning a trade which they did not really like. A

15

further irritation was the restriction of free movement, imposed on the students by the French authorities; even for going into the village, a pass was required. All these restrictions were entirely unnecessary, as refugees anywhere else were able to move about freely.

Of course, students did not have any worries about renewing their permits, which normally had to be done periodically with endless visits to the authorities and no way of knowing whether an extension would be granted, as no permanent asylum was ever given. Nor did they have to worry about getting money to keep them going, although a hunger strike was instrumental in obtaining ten francs pocket money a week.

Another problem was the lack of girls, as there were only married couples at the Centre and only three girls in the village. Not an ideal situation. My own position in the Centre was not an easy one. I did not know any of the students and I had to gain their confidence in my day-to-day contacts as many thought that I was part of the Committee which administered the Centre, and not a refugee myself.

The fact that my Director took me with him wherever he went so that I could liaise, did not help. Nevertheless, I learnt to be equally loyal to the students and to the administration which had asked me to undertake this job, by examining each problem with an open mind. As the confidence of the students grew, the number of personal interviews I was asked for became so numerous that I had to set time aside each night to listen and try to assist with the many problems.

These ranged from enquiries about the possibilities of further emigration to other countries and the chances of making a living there, enquiries about lost members of their families, requests for books and other articles needed, health problems etc. to quite trivial matters which became important because of the isolation in which most of the students found themselves.

However, by July 1939, everything was running smoothly and a very good relationship had been built up with the local French population. On Bastille-Day, July 14th, the entire Centre went to the War Memorial in Martigny-les-Bains to pay homage to the war-dead and deposited a wreath. Meanwhile our garden experts had arranged a beautiful flower bed with vividly coloured flowers spelling out "Vive la France".

I had planned a special, very festive lunch and our cooks had worked all night to make a success of it. Our Director made a very moving speech in French, which I had to translate. This went off very well.

For the evening the Centre had planned a special event. The local theatre had been hired and the entire village was invited to a Variety Performance, thought out and presented by the artistically inclined members of the Centre. This was much appreciated by the villagers and the many guests of honour who came, even though some of it was presented in heavy Viennese dialect. During the interval the students had prepared a gigantic firework display in the adjoining park. This is traditional in French villages on July 14th, usually provided by the Lord of the Manor.

The following day we again invited the village to a dance, for which we had prepared a buffet with over 700 delicious sandwiches and I had obtained free of charge, a great many bottles of wine and spirits for their and our entertainment from the various grocers serving the Centre. At midnight a large number of doughnuts provided by our boys made their welcome appearance.

It was a well deserved break for the students and an excellent opportunity to get to know the people of the village and to foster good relations with them. None of us suspected at that time all this would come to an abrupt ending in less than 7 weeks with the outbreak of World War II, on September 3rd 1939!

I had burned the midnight oil for a number of nights in preparation for the festivities and had decided to get up late the following morning. However, at 8 o'clock I was woken up and told that the Sous-Prefect of the region had arrived unexpectedly in gala uniform in order to have a look at the Centre! I had no time to get dressed and I just had to receive him in my pyjamas. It must surely have been the first time that he was thus received! The contrast between his Gala Uniform and my night-attire reminded me of a comedy series, or perhaps "The Good Soldier Schwejk". The Sous-Prefect was duly impressed with what we were doing and I think that the Centre would have fulfilled its purpose, had it been allowed to continue.

CHAPTER
THREE

However, as mentioned, it came to an abrupt ending with the declaration of war, though it turned out to have been a good preparation for the difficult years to come.

The Sous-Prefect whom we had impressed so much did not lose any time to get all the students, and of course my colleagues and myself interned. Married couples were naturally separated and for them it must have been much worse than for single men. With our luggage duly stored — never to be seen again — we were put into some old coaches and could only take a minimum of things with us. I have no idea what happened to all the equipment which we left behind at the Hotel International, but I later wished I could have taken my mattress along, because from then on straw-sacks were the order of the day.

It does not require much imagination to understand the indignity and the outrage of such treatment, in other words to be put in one melting pot — and in fact to be interned with — our own enemies, i.e. German Nazis, who at that time were still living in France.

The French never took the trouble to sort them out or to separate us from them. Here we were then, having fled to France between 1933 when Hitler came to power and 1938, having been subjected to all sorts of difficulties and chicaneries as to status, residential permits, or any chance to earn a living as refugees from Nazi oppression. Now suddenly, we were no longer refugees, but Germans and considered "enemies"! We just could not understand what was going on, surely by now it must have been clear to all that we were on their side! Soon, we imagined, reason must prevail and we would be able to join the French Army and fight the common enemy! But such an offer never came.

When the Germans invaded France, in June 1940, they found their own people still together in the same camp with those who had fled Germany many years before!

I think that all refugees from Nazism in France during the first days of war must have felt the same sense of anger and frustration as the students and I did when we were suddenly thrown into an internment camp, and worse still together with non-refugees, usually ferocious Nazis! After all, Hitler was our enemy long before war was declared on him by the Allies. Because of him and his murderous henchmen, we had to leave our country of birth, our homes, our professions or occupations and, frequently, also our families.

We had to battle not only with a new language, but also with the many difficulties the authorities constantly put in our way, and very few of us were ever allowed to

20

earn our living in France and had to rely on charities for our support, which did nothing to boost our morale.

Suddenly we were in the same position as the Nazis themselves — "Enemy Aliens"!

We thus had many difficulties to overcome, breaking bread, so to speak, with our enemies in the camp, but looking back on it now I would say that our indignation and frustration with the French and their total unwillingness to even try to enlist our services against the common foe was the greater burden to bear.

Our new "home" for some time to be was "Le camp du Châtelet" in Neufchâteau (Vosges). It was a blessing we had not been living in the lap of luxury at the Centre, otherwise the sudden drop in the conveniences available at the camp would have been more difficult to bear.

I was now one of the internees, no longer able to assist the others with their problems, as I shared the same myself. No longer enjoying the privilege of my own room, albeit without running water or heating, was perhaps one of the most difficult things to get used to, as apart from brief periods in my early hotel career, I never shared a room with anyone. Naturally, my very busy daily routine, which I had got used to in the months past, made the transition to camp life where there was no activity of any sort rather more difficult to adjust to.

Camps, whether they are internment or prisoner-of-war camps, have an atmosphere of their own, which is dictated by the fellow prisoners and the local circumstances, as well as the treatment by the

21

authorities. Food, or rather the lack of it, becomes increasingly important. If there is enough food, the meal becomes an important and integral part of one's existence; if there is none or too little, it becomes the most important item of conversation with everyone making up menus of what they would like to eat. This was the first of many camps I was to know during the next seven years, fortunately not all of them with barbed wire around them. It takes some time to get used to that sort of life, especially if one has been a very private person and did not have to share basic facilities. Then the fact that one is deprived of one's liberty without having committed a crime slowly sinks in. The world inside the camp becomes the measure of one's horizon, unless one is able to exercise one's mind beyond the limits of the camp's confine.

Conversation with fellow-prisoners on all sorts of subjects is a great help, but time lies heavy on one's hands as week after week passes by without anyone having the slightest idea what the future has in store. A prisoner knows at least how long he has to spend behind bars; we, at that time and even later, did not have a clue. The French never gave us the opportunity to join the Army, but I was determined not to rot in the camp forever. It was then I made up my mind to find my way to England somehow; after all my family were there and I considered it my duty to do something positive for the war effort. Little did I know then that it would take me until the autumn of 1943 to reach my goal!

The period between the outbreak of war and the invasion of France, in May 1940, was known as the "phoney war" when nothing much happened.

Some of our fellow internees who obtained "affidavits" from their relatives in the United States, were given a visa and left via Portugal, to our great joy. There was no envy, although those of us who remained behind were sure we would never be able to leave.

We changed camps several times. The last camp before the German invasion was a disused mill somewhere in Northern France. I remember the dust and filth which greeted us on arrival. Our bed was a sack filled with straw on a concrete floor and no room to move between the sacks. As in the first camp, there were no recreational facilities whatsoever. No books, radio or newspapers. Fortunately the mill stream gave us the opportunity to swim.

Even then, the French had not once offered us participation in the war against Hitler. We were still housed together with Nazi Germans.

CHAPTER
FOUR

The "Phoney War" went on as before until we detected a certain excitement among our guards.

It was May 10 1940. The Germans had invaded the Netherlands. The rest is history. Obviously, the fear of falling into their hands again struck terror into our hearts.

France has the Maginot Line, some said; others did not have much faith in it. As the days passed, there could be little doubt that France would fall as well. The crushing war-machine which the Germans had unleashed, the large number of tanks and the Stukas, appeared to be unstoppable.

The Allies, having waited for the war to start in earnest after the long months of "Phoney War", were taken by surprise at the rapid progress of the German Army. After King Leopold surrendered Belgium, the fate of France, in spite of all the preparations, seemed sealed. The British Expeditionary Force in northern France was in danger of being wiped out by the rapid German advance.

The French, apparently wishing to make it impossible for any refugees to escape before the inevitable arrival of the Germans, took all our footwear away! Even had we wanted to flee, it would have been extremely difficult, if not impossible at that time, as one expected the Germans to occupy the whole of France. It was not to be the last time that the French were handing refugees to the Germans on a platter, as this narrative will show later on. Great anxiety as to our fate arose among us with every rumour which reached us.

We all knew that we could not run away, even if we would have had our footwear. In which direction could one go, given that the French guards would have let us go? They wanted to make a good impression on the Germans and were even more on their guard at that time, so that they would be able to hand us over with not one internee missing from their lists! And when they came on the 22nd of June 1940, it was just like that.

In the camp we had no idea what happened at Dunkerque, even after the arrival of the Germans; they had never mentioned it. When we were given English loaves of bread and other obviously British food in tins, we knew these rations had been captured. We were wondering whether the same had happened to the British Army or whether they were able to escape before the Germans reached them.

We were fortunate in as far as only the German army reached our camp and they did not have much time for us. Had it been an "SS" regiment it would have been a different story.

For a while things went on as before. Our shoes magically reappeared after a few days. By now German soldiers were strutting through the camp, telling us that by the next day German Railways would run regular trains to Paris and cheering us up with other depressing news. Soon the non-Jewish Germans left to join the army, but no decision had apparently been made about us. We were waiting daily to be sent to a concentration camp in Germany, but instead we were sent north to yet another camp in France, in Clisson near Nantes, where the Germans were in total command.

When we arrived we found a variety of Allied internees, English and Canadians among them, all civilians. The Germans thought that they were soldiers in disguise, as they continued asking them for their rank, army number etc. Soon some members of the "SS" arrived, but to our great surprise they were more interested in showing us how to dig holes for lamp-posts and trenches for sewage. I soon found myself excavating a deep 14″ square hole for a lamp-post with a pneumatic drill, and as I had to stand in this hole at least up to my navel I was forced to stand on one foot, so as not to bore holes into my toes instead of into the rock. Fortunately, there was not always petrol for the generator, and in consequence work proceeded slowly. Of course, this meant that I had to work on the trenches, which was really exhausting on the rations we received, especially if one was not used to work with a shovel.

Immediately after Dunkerque the Germans had neither the time for, nor any interest in, civilian internees and it was lucky for us refugees from Nazi Germany that we were in the same camp as the Allied internees, caught by the Germans when they overran

26

France. Our Camp Commandant was an army-man of the older generation and very soon after their arrival the "SS" men were sent somewhere else. Nevertheless, we feared that any day the Jewish contingent would be sent to Germany, the Germans only needed time to organize themselves after the fall of France.

Meanwhile, life in the camp settled down to a daily routine. Although we did not share a hut with other nationalities, who were all housed separately, we were meeting English, Canadians and other Allied internees in the compound of the camp.

I can still see a group of Canadian theologians, for instance, taking their daily walk at a very fast pace from one perimeter to the other, always engaged in debates on religious matters. In order to enable as many as possible to participate in this physical and mental exercise, half the group walked backwards facing the forward walking group, thus when they came to the perimeter they just had to march back to the other side, without anyone having to turn round; this struck me as very ingenious.

I suppose we each had our own fears and futile desires. As far as the Allied internees were concerned, they seemed to accept this situation and were not frightfully worried one way or the other. Of course, they had only been in camp for a short while, having been picked up by the Germans, or more likely the French, after the invasion of France. They also knew that they were protected by the Geneva Convention in the same way as Prisoners-of-War. As to us, with every day that passed, our fear of being sent to a concentration camp in Germany — nothing was known as yet of extermination camps — was growing. Surely, when news would be filtering through to Berlin of our presence in the camp, the inevitable must soon happen.

One day the Feldwebel in charge of the Guard ordered me to come with him. He had his rifle over his shoulder which was unusual and he made for the gate. Where was he taking me? Was I being transferred to yet another camp, and why just me? We were walking outside the camp by now and still he was not volunteering any information. Finally I could not stand the suspense any longer, and I asked him in German where he was taking me, "Einkaufen" was his answer. To go shopping! So he wanted someone to carry his shopping. I was relieved. However, when we entered the first shop the real reason for having taken me with him became clear; I was supposed to interpret for him. I found myself in a very embarrassing position as I have no foreign accent in French. I did not want the shopkeeper to think that I was a collaborator, especially as I had to bargain over the price, and I therefore told them that I was an internee at the nearby camp, whereupon they usually released a stream of abuse against all German soldiery, which even the Feldwebel could not fail to sense, although the expressions used by the shopkeepers were not immediately clear to him.

In spite of all this, our first outing must have been a success as the shopping expeditions were often repeated and I came to the conclusion that the Feldwebel must either have a large family or be engaged in the black market. As long as he paid for the goods, I did not care either way. For me, these afternoon outings certainly were a relief from the strenuous physical work I would have had to do in camp.

By this time I became very concerned about my family in England from whom I had not heard since the German invasion of France. They could not possibly have any idea where I was, or whether I was still alive. I had written all the postcards we were allowed and was hoping that these would reach them, which in fact they did, as I found out much later.

CHAPTER
FIVE

In mid-October 1941 orders were suddenly given for the Jews to pack their belongings and prepare for departure the next day. One can easily imagine our feelings. Here we were, comparatively comfortable, protected somehow by the presence of Allied internees and under a military command which so far had not given us a great deal of trouble. What lay ahead? Where would they send us? Nobody knew the answer.

The following morning, October 18th 1940, a train drew up outside the camp. With it had come a detachment of the most vicious troops I had encountered so far. Their behaviour was most frightening, constantly shouting, pushing and threatening, accompanied by anti-Semitic remarks and abuse. We had already been standing for ages, lined up outside on the sand, as there was, of course, no station. Guards were eyeing us grimly, waiting for someone to move out of line or to say something.

As we could not communicate with one another, we were left with our own thoughts and tried to look straight ahead without attracting the attention of our guards.

At last, a whistle and a stringent command gave us the order to board the train. What a relief! It took some time before the embarkation was completed as they obviously wanted to have their fun with us, and we were scared to death; the only way to stay out of trouble was not to open one's mouth and to do what they asked. Finally, we moved off without any rations and clutching our few belongings, which in my case included an old typewriter, an Underwood portable, given to me earlier in the war by one of the fortunate people who were able to leave for the United States when there was still time. In fact, this typewriter had been commandeered by the German Commandant earlier on, but using some silly excuse I got it back into my possession just before we were leaving the camp. I was still using it in 1999 when I changed to a word processor. The *Old Faithful* will now find a new home in a museum, as it must be at least eighty years old. The only other possession which I had, and which the Germans never found on me, was the gold watch and fob given to me by my father. These two items assumed great importance later in the war, as the fob was instrumental in my reaching England and thus freedom and the watch played a vital part in meeting Lili, my wife-to-be.

To get back to the train though; it was impossible to guess in what direction we were travelling as there was no sun that day and we did not pass any familiar towns or places. It was generally assumed that we were going eastwards towards the German border. The train stopped frequently although no-one got off or on, only the shouting of the guards and their abuse could be heard. The night before we had no time to ponder how this sudden decision to move us had come about and who was responsible for it, the Military or the "SS", or was it on special orders from Berlin? Now all these questions rose to the fore and speculation was rife.

We had been going for several hours, it was almost nightfall. Nothing to eat, nothing to drink, but that was the least of our worries. Was I now being taken back to Germany from where I had fled seven and a half years ago? They had already caught up with me in France and somewhere here I still saw a ray of hope, but Germany — that would be the end!

Suddenly the train stopped to shouts of "Raus, Raus!" which is German for "out". It was dark by then. The train had stopped at a siding, nowhere near a station, and we started wondering if we were just again being transferred to another camp. Luckily I had managed to stay in the same compartment with three friends of mine — Konrad Bieber whom I had known in Paris before the war, Otto Seligmann without whose help later on this book may not have been written, as he was instrumental in providing me with a "carte d'identité", and Erwin Roos who came from Strasbourg. There was no time to think, just to gather the bit of luggage one had, in my case all in a sack, and to line up outside as the Germans commanded.

Plenty of insults followed; fortunately we all kept quiet, otherwise I am sure they would have used their rifle-butts. After a while we were driven off on foot and I mean that literally. Out on a dark road, illuminated only by the lights of the motorcycles with side-cars, with two Germans armed to the teeth in each, constantly shouting, urging us to march faster. I could hardly carry my sack which was so heavy, because of my typewriter.

There were so many of us and for the first time I discovered that there was a group of Arabs who had been interned in a camp near to ours, but with whom we had had no contact. They were mostly peddlers from Paris and other parts, who in peacetime would try to sell you carpets, rugs, beads and the like, and who had been rounded up either by the Germans or more likely by the French themselves. Suddenly we heard the Germans shouting in a sneering way: "Now Mandel can have you!"

George Mandel, a Jew, had been the Minister for the Interior before the fall of France and we knew that he had escaped to North Africa from Vichy, only to be brought back and interned later. We hardly believed what we heard! Were they pushing us off into the non-occupied part of France? Before we knew where we were, they suddenly turned round on their motorbikes, yelling some more insults and were gone. We found ourselves all alone and in a most confused state.

My friends and I had succeeded in staying together and we hastily discussed what to do in the new situation. There was only one thing to do, we decided. Wherever we were, we quickly had to get away from the throng, especially from the Arabs, as it was obvious to us that they would steal our meagre belongings as soon as they sensed that there was no authority about. This we heard later was exactly what they did to the others, very cleverly too, as they did not take their cases which would have been evidence, but just slit them open and took what they fancied from their contents. It was all so fast and so unexpected, we were told, that nothing could be done about it.

By now we were almost sure that we had been dispatched into the unoccupied zone of France by the Germans. What we could not understand was how it was possible that there was not a soul on the border, or anyone to receive such a large contingent of people. Much later we were to learn that the Germans did in fact inform the authorities in the so-called "free zone" of this human consignment being sent south, but somehow the French got the place muddled or the Germans deliberately sent us to another place than the one convened. Apparently a number of lorries had waited elsewhere to put us in yet another camp.

What made the German High Command decide to get rid of us in the first place? Most probably with the logistic problems in 1940, shortly after the occupation of France, they could not see why they should feed us when the French could do so. Their plans for slave-labour and the extermination of the Jews were not far advanced enough at that time and I have no doubt that this saved our lives. Also they must have reckoned that they could get us back any time they wanted.

However, at this dramatic moment the four of us did not stop to ponder on these questions. We only had one thought in mind and that was to get lost before anyone else could get hold of us. So we went off into the darkness and made sure that no-one was following us. After ten minutes or so we came upon a barn and decided to spend the night in it, keeping very quiet, and to continue early the following morning. Being used to sleeping on hard straw, we found the hay a nice change, hoping that none of us would get a sneezing attack.

Next morning, before we had a chance to wake up properly, the farmer came into the barn and discovered our presence.

As far as we were concerned, the French people of the "free zone" would be only too glad to welcome us with open arms and we found our farmer was indeed very friendly, allowing us to stay in his barn and inviting us for supper that night. We felt so happy as only free men can, after a long period of confinement. However, this newly found freedom was not to last.

In the evening we all trouped into the farmhouse, having cleaned ourselves up as best we could. The farmer's wife was busy preparing the meal and the pleasant cooking smells made our mouths water. The table was laid and all was anticipation. It was the first time since the outbreak of war that any one of us had sat at a table in congenial surroundings, let alone in a family.

Apparently there was another guest to come, because we observed one surplus cover. Suddenly the door opened and a man in the uniform of an officer of the Gendarmerie Nationale appeared on the doorstep. We immediately thought the obvious, that he had come to arrest us.

But not so, he sat down to have dinner with us as a friend of the family, or so we believed. The conversation was fluent during dinner as our hosts wanted to know what had happened to us. Little did we realise that this was our first and last meal with our new-found-friend. In fact, we had figured that we could ask him for work on the farm which would have solved our immediate problem!

However, before we had a chance to tuck into whatever cheese was to close the meal, a number of other gendarmes arrived and it was explained to us, gently, I must say, that we had to take our kit and go with them. We had no idea what had happened to the others, but we had a feeling that we would soon be together with them again. It looked as if our escapade was just a very short respite.

It was now obvious that the farmer had given us away and told the Gendarmerie of his find; we were surprised that they had not come sooner. We were not very pleased, but what could we do but to thank the farmer and his wife for the meal. Soon we found ourselves under escort in some vehicle and then we arrived at some military barracks in the town of Montauban in the second half of October 1940. The others were nowhere to be seen.

CHAPTER
SIX

In consequence, the obvious solution for the French was to enrol us all into what was known as the "Prestataires", a sort of Pioneer Corps for foreigners, and that was how we became members of the "302ième Compagnie des Travailleurs Etrangés" and were sent to a barrack-camp outside the little village of Septfonds in the Department of Tarn et Garonne. This was to be my "home" for almost three years until I went into hiding on the first leg of my journey to freedom and to England in 1943.

I have never understood if the "Prestataires" were supposed to be part of the army as only some of us had uniforms and all our officers — or were they overseers with the exception of the Camp Commandant — were civilians. There was military discipline with parades and hoisting of the flag, passes and all outward trimmings of military life, but what it boiled down to really was that we provided cheap labour for the farmers and others who wanted our services. The rest of the time we just moped about, performing fairly useless tasks which again made me think that we might have been part of the Army.

The Quarters of "302 Compagnie des Travailleurs Etrangés" at Septfonds were the worst I had seen so far. The wooden huts, freezing in winter and boiling in summer, were erected on sand without a concrete floor, hence the fleas. If I would be asked what I remember most vividly of my sojourn in the camp at Septfonds, it would be those fleas, which plagued us night after night. I had never had any close contact with fleas before, let alone hundreds of them. It was quite impossible to kill them and all one could do was to persuade them to jump into water, provided they were inclined to do so and obliged. However, this was not possible when one was lying under a blanket, trying to get some sleep; the only thing which helped were mothballs, which they hate. We slept on double bunks on straw-sacks with straw-pillows. Although fleas can jump high, I always found that the lower bunks were much more popular with them; judging by the blood they sucked out of us every night, they should have had the strength to jump to the ceiling.

For washing and shaving we had running cold water outside the huts, fine in summer and horrible in winter. There were no proper showers and no baths. During rainy periods the camp was full of mud.

The food was never adequate and was eaten in those horrible barracks, among the fleas, out of tin plates. At least our boys were allowed to cook it and they did their best with what they were given. Surprisingly, in spite of these conditions, I cannot remember anyone being seriously ill.

Our spirits were usually high, but it became abundantly clear, as time marched on, that we were going nowhere fast. Those with connections tried successfully sometimes, but usually without success, to obtain an immigration visa for the United States, which in spite of our conscription into the "Prestataire Service" was still possible.

Meanwhile all avenues which might eventually allow one to leave the un-occupied zone of France which the Germans were bound to overrun sooner or later, had to be explored. I had already been registered for immigration with the American Consulate in Paris before the war and I now asked them to transfer my dossier to Marseille. The next step was to obtain an affidavit, which was required by law for all immigrants. This is a financial guarantee by a person living in the United States who has sufficient means not only to look after himself and his family, but also any prospective immigrant whom he or she has sponsored. My parents in England were instrumental in obtaining three affidavits, two from cousins and one from a friend of my father. When I heard that these had arrived at the Consulate in Marseille my hopes were high and I immediately asked for permission to go there. I knew that even if I was given a visa, I would also need an exit permit from France — always supposing that my release from the "Prestataires" would be granted. Furthermore, I would have to find a passage on one of the very few passenger boats still plying the Atlantic during war-time from Marseille, where apparently hundreds of other refugees were already desperately waiting for passages, or go via Lisbon for which transit visas for Spain and Portugal were required. I decided that in a situation like mine no stone must be left unturned.

Of course it would be senseless to obtain these documents before a visa was granted because they had a limited validity, and in any case, confirmation from the American Consulate would have been necessary to the effect that I really had been granted an immigration visa.

How to obtain all these documents from Camp Septfonds and how to acquire the passage money of about 500 dollars was still a mystery to me.

There seemed to be little point in worrying and weighing up hypothetical impossibilities at that moment.

As I was queueing outside the Consulate in April 1941, together with a large number of other hopefuls, I heard it said that Admiral William D. Leahy, the American Ambassador to France, had been given instructions to be much stricter with immigration from France. In fact, no U.S. visa could be issued by the Consulate until the State Department in Washington had sanctioned it. I could well believe it, when my turn came to see an official inside the Consulate. Only the affidavit from my cousins had arrived. I was informed that I should obtain supplementary affidavits, because this one was not strong enough. In order to demonstrate the difficulties which confronted would-be immigrants during a period when their lives were at stake, it is worth noting the many obstacles put in their way at that time. I could hardly believe it when the consular official told me what was required:

- Declaration that nothing had changed since the affidavit was first issued.
- A letter from my cousins' employer to the effect that they were still employed and would be in the future.
- Federal Income returns by my cousins for the years 1939 and 1940.
- A moral and political affidavit given to them by an American citizen.
- Replies to the famous "13 points" of assurances which immigrants had to give.

Needless to say, none of this came to any fruition before the Germans occupied the then still free zone, including Marseille.

It is now well known that the United States was not the only country making it difficult for Jewish refugees to enter, but many were fortunate enough to be admitted and their lives were saved. It is difficult for anyone who was not in France at that time to imagine that the possession of an American visa, in the great majority of cases, meant the difference between life and death in the gas chambers! Even before the occupation of the so-called "free zone" by the Germans in 1942, the French had interned a great many Jewish refugees in the various camps, such as "Le Vernet" and "Gurs", and due to the conditions of the armistice between Vichy-France and Germany, the Germans could demand the delivery of any refugees into their hands at any time. In fact, a German commission went round all the camps, but at that time they apparently were not interested in the ordinary non-political Jewish refugees, the majority of whom could have been saved if other Western countries would have admitted them more freely.

As it was, once the Germans occupied the "free zone" in November 1942, it was too late; after a while deportations to the extermination camps began and the opportunity to save these lives which was undoubtedly there before, was lost for ever on December 10th, when Hitler ordered the arrests and deportations of ALL Jews from France.

CHAPTER
SEVEN

But back to the camp at Septfonds. Captain Prévot, our Camp Commandant, although a martinet in all matters and more feared than respected by most as a total collaborator with Vichy, soon discovered that there was a lot of talent among his "Prestataires" and started to organise us into performing groups. To further his aims he even permitted rehearsals in working hours. We organised variety shows and concerts, first in the camp with invited guests and later in various other places, such as Montauban and Toulouse, where we also produced ourselves on the radio. This was the one and only time I was requested to sing on radio, when before, under the bathroom shower was the more likely place! Our variety shows were really a lot of fun and made everyone laugh. I usually acted as compère because of my fluent French and played in the sketches which we thought out ourselves.

There were 50 members and I had also to act as Secretary, making sure that we were ready to go anywhere at a moment's notice. Quite often we played for the benefit of French Prisoners of War. On one of our visits to Toulouse we had two performances in the largest theatre there and performed twice on the radio.

The shows usually lasted for several hours and sometimes did not finish until the early morning.

We were not paid for this or any other work we did, unless we were detached to a farmer who would pay us, as for instance later when we were sent on detachment in the vineyards.

In between, I was giving English lessons to the daughter of one of our officers and at the same time I had to look after his rabbits, for which I was rewarded with a cup of coffee and some bread and butter, which was more appreciated than money at that time.

As already mentioned, our food rations were never sufficient and soon little stoves made out of empty tins and fed with small pieces of dry wood were used by most of us to supplement our food with anything cookable, which was not much. We usually took Soya flour, which was not rationed and with which one could make a soup, improved by some onions and carrots if one could find them. Then we made jam with apricots and saccharine.

I spent most of my free time at the local grocery shop which belonged to an elderly lady, Mademoiselle Miquel. At first I went there to see whether I could persuade her to let me have a little chocolate, some sugar or perhaps even some butter, but then we spent hours discussing all sorts of things and I started to enjoy our meetings, especially when she offered me a cup of real coffee and a biscuit. As time passed she could be persuaded to sell me some chocolate and other goodies, not otherwise available, and I have never forgotten the kindness and understanding for my situation which she showed me during these years. Fortunately I was later able to reciprocate her kindness in a small way by sending cocoa from England which she desperately wanted.

It is difficult to imagine now what importance food or the lack of it assumed in one's life at that time. One was constantly hungry and I remember cycling twenty miles every week-end in the hope — not the certainty — of obtaining another loaf of bread from a baker who once had been kind enough to let me have one; bread was, of course, rationed in France. In consequence, to this day I cannot bear to throw bread away, even when it has become stale.

In 1941 I was very lucky to be able to visit my uncle and aunt who lived in Nice. In fact, I was able to go there several times on leave during my time in Septfonds and these visits provided the only lighter moments of my life in France, during the war. My uncle and aunt were both very depressed, as they had an American visa but could not get away to join their sons who were already in the U.S.A., because they were unable to obtain the necessary French exit permit. However, I always managed to cheer them up and to show them how wonderful life in Nice was in comparison to other parts of France, especially the occupied zone. After all there was a war on, but in Nice it was difficult to imagine it. Apart from the food rationing which was as severe as everywhere else, life went on pretty much as it always had on the Côte d'Azure. The cafés were full and the restaurants were busy, even if one had to give up one's coupons for meat. The vegetable and flower markets were just as busy as in peace-time. The Promenade des Anglais was full of people sunning themselves; one was simply not aware that there was a war on.

When I returned in British uniform, shortly after the Armistice in 1945, also on leave, and probably the only British soldier in town, as Nice was occupied by the Americans, things were very different. I had failed to take the precaution of making any arrangements for food. Not wanting to touch the meagre rations of my uncle and aunt and not having any ration card myself, I really went hungry and I had to go to the Red Cross for some emergency tins and once I got myself a meal at the Hotel Negresco where the Americans were billeted. The French Colonel in charge of the hotel then was still manager when I revisited the hotel again in 1978 in very different circumstances!

During my visit in 1945, I was of course in uniform and I remember one day I decided to thumb a lift to the Italian border, just past Menton, and to go into Italy as far as San Remo, which I knew well, having worked there three winter seasons as receptionist in the Hotel Astoria Westend before the war. Nobody asked me for any papers at the frontier which I found odd, but then I observed that most people simply ignored it and I thought to myself what a wonderful idea if this would always be so. Having passed the same border post in 1983 I was pleased to observe that we were waved through without having to show any passports or car documents. I remembered that day in 1945 and was glad that we have now become "one happy European family", at least in tourism, compared with the pre-war years and the many post-war years when a frontier crossing was very formal and could take a long time. One can only hope that people do not abuse this improvement and spoil it again for all.

As to our work in the camp, we were usually detailed to assist either some farmers in the region or to cut wood in the forest. However, in September 1941, a detachment of 115 of us were sent further south to assist with "les vendanges", the picking of grapes and the making of wine. This turned out to be a rather enjoyable experience. We were all assigned to individual winegrowers. At first I was sent to Lansargues in the Department Herault. Having reported to our farmer and having been introduced to his family, three of us were assigned three straw mattresses in a sort of spare room, with a kitchenette. It was a lot better than what we were used to from our barracks in Septfonds. I think the farmer was mighty pleased that I spoke fluent French, the rest he could teach us as we went along.

So on my first night there I was dreaming of the culinary delights which would await me during my stay with them! What I had not reckoned with was that in the Herault Department everyone was concentrating on vineyards and nobody had ever given any thought to growing vegetables or fruit or for that matter to keeping food-producing animals, not even poultry.

The result was that for the next six weeks we were living on just four kinds of food — tinned sardines, bread, grapes and wine — nothing else. No food ever seemed to reach the Department from elsewhere. It would seem that all the necessary vitamins and minerals are contained in these foods and that they held sufficient calories to sustain one.

In the Herault, grapes are picked when ripe, not over-ripe. Next morning 1 became a carrier, whose job it is to carry the large wooden caskets into which the grapes picked by the others are tipped. The casket is then carried on one's back with shoulder-straps. Once it is full, one has to empty it into a two-wheel cart, stepping on a ladder with this casket on one's back and tip it over one's head into the cart. This may sound easy, but it is not quite as easy as it sounds, because if one is not skilled at this performance, the grape juice, which has already formed in abundance through the sheer weight of the grapes in the casket, trickles down one's neck and makes the whole back, bottom and legs sticky; a very nasty feeling! In addition there is the problem of balancing on top of the ladder and if one is very clumsy one gets one's hair washed in grape juice.

The wine produced in the Herault Department, which is not so well-known outside France, is good and is between what is known as "vin du pays" and "vin d'appellation controlé".

Meanwhile I was sent to Landerrouat in the Gironde region which was quite a different story. The farmers there had always been growing vegetables as well as grapes and kept farm animals, which made it possible for them to have a more varied diet during the war when everything was rationed and no transport available. So we had chickens, ducks and hare, bread and butter and heaps of potatoes. I also slept in a proper bed. In the Gironde, where most of the claret comes from, grapes not only ripen later as a rule, but are left until they are over-ripe and have accumulated the maximum amount of natural sugar. When I got there they were nearly ready for picking and it was a good thing that we did not have to rely on these grapes for food, as they were too far gone to be eaten.

After a couple of weeks of picking, I was detailed to the distillation department where pure, or nearly pure, alcohol is distilled from the residue of the grapes after pressing. When the residue comes from the presses it is stored underground for fermentation. My job was to see to just that. When I started to investigate the situation, I discovered that whoever had worked there before me had simply dropped the residue through the storage hole, which was similar to, but larger than, the holes still to be found in London streets for coal-cellars. Thus there was a huge mountain piling up to the top of the hole and already fermenting. No-one had thought of distributing the masses all over the cellar. I went to work with a large pitchfork, standing on top of that mountain and started shifting it, trying to keep my head out of the hole so as to be able to breathe! This was dreadful work, as the fumes kept getting at me especially when I had to bend down in order to get the stuff shifted. Although I never became intoxicated by them, alcohol-fumes, even from surgical spirit, still irritate me today, and make me cough. But worse was to come when I heard that all the alcohol already distilled had been requisitioned by the German

Army for war purposes. This really knocked me sideways.

For my own benefit, I had earlier on lowered my French Army "bidon" (a military water bottle) into the alcohol-storage-tank with the help of a long string and made myself a very neat brandy with it. After hearing what the ultimate destination of the contents of the tank was going to be, my "bidon" made many trips down the tank and was then emptied into a gully; so at least some of its contents did not reach the Germans. Generally speaking, the time spent in the vineyards was a happy one and I would certainly recommend it to any young person today.

We had been away nine weeks in all and for the first time we had been paid. Everyone of us received 50 Francs a day, less 15 Francs for food, the wine not being charged, of course, as it came out of taps — one red the other white — under which one could lie and just open one's mouth if one felt so inclined.

CHAPTER
EIGHT

On the way back to camp, having saved all the money I had earned, I decided to spend a couple of accumulated free days in Montauban where I was given a room with central heating in the hotel. Both the hotel and the central heating were a fantastic luxury after the rigours I had gone through. I made use of these days to look for a job, maybe in an hotel as after all this was my profession. I even managed to find one, but permission for a detachment from camp was never given.

When we returned to camp in the middle of November, the conditions there were even harder to bear after the time spent in the vineyards. However, soon afterwards, "Radio Toulouse" engaged our choir for just one performance and that provided the last bit of fun we were going to have. I can still see us now, being installed for the night in the barracks in Toulouse, which were a lot better than our huts at "Septfonds" and I can still hear the announcer presenting the choir of the "Travailleurs Etrangérs"! I suppose we must have cheered up a housewife or two, who might have been listening.

In January 1942 I had acquired a second-hand bike which made my life a lot more interesting, as I could get further away on it and visit my friends in Montauban on a week-end pass. Thus I had a certain mobility, which was not only enabling me to spend my free time outside the camp, but also made it possible, later on, to save my life.

As emigration to the U.S.A. was to remain a pipe-dream for the time being, I was certainly not giving up hope to realise my main objective, rejoining my family in England and enlisting in the British Army, which at that time was even more of a pipe-dream than a visa for America! My first move in this direction was to get a job outside the camp to which I would then be detached. I had a feeling, having gone through this experience once before, that the French would hand us over on a platter into German hands, should the Germans take it into their heads to occupy the whole country. As it happened, it worked out exactly that way and my one idea at that time was to be as far away from the camp as possible, when this happened!

The American Quakers had an office in nearby Montauban and following some strong recommendations from the English Quakers who had taken the Jewish refugees in Farnham, Surrey, including my parents, under their wing, I obtained a twelve-months contract in July 1942. I was hoping to leave camp soon and had already obtained my civilian ration cards on the strength of that contract, when I heard that permission was not given for my working outside. I was just about to return my ration-cards which, of course, I had not used, when a detachment of gendarmes descended on the camp, the first sign of possible interference with our lives. They found my ration-cards which landed me in the camp's prison, awaiting a decision as to whether I would be prosecuted for possessing them. My only worry was that the Germans might come during that time and I would be trapped. Fortunately, as none of the ration coupons were used, I was returned to the barracks after some weeks. By then I realised that there was little time left to organise an escape route, if I could not get a detachment.

In fact, shortly before the Allied landing in North Africa in November 1942, the French surrounded our Prestataire camp with gendarmes, so as to neatly hand us over to the Germans when they occupied the whole of France, after the landing.

I had an inkling of what they had in mind and before the first gendarme had arrived I hopped on my bicycle and cycled to a nearby farmhouse where I had made arrangements previously for just such a contingency. This was not an easy decision to make, as I knew I could not simply return to camp, even after only one day's absence. They would no doubt be looking for me. The fact that my hide-out was so near the camp, was no advantage either.

At that time I owned a lovely German shepherd bitch called "Dolly" who never left my side, although I could not feed her because there was nothing to feed her with, but my friends in the kitchen managed somehow to sustain her every day. I had to find a home for her before I went into hiding of course, but she sensed that I would never come back and was howling piteously when I finally left her at her new home. I think we both felt our parting ways for a long time after.

I had also left my typewriter in the village with Mme. Miquel from where it was collected by a friend after the war. I did not see Mme. Miquel again, although we corresponded after the liberation of France, but I never forgot all the kindness shown and the help she had given to me. In fact, the couple who owned the farm were cousins of Mme. Miquel and were of the tough breed of French people who were willing to help against the common enemy, the Germans and the Vichy Government.

It can be said that every Jew who survived in France during that difficult period owed his or her life to French people who either assisted them or kept quiet or both; and that in the last resort distinguishes the individual Frenchman and woman from the official policy of the Vichy Government, which was to get rid of Jews one way or another and to assist the Germans to the fullest possible extent, even before they were asked.

The one condition for my hiding there was that I had to stay in bed all day so that nobody would see me, and if someone should ask questions, I would be a cousin who was ill in bed and could not be disturbed! However, I had not promised to stay in bed at night and one night my curiosity as to what had happened in the camp got the better of me. So without anyone at the farm being aware of it, I took myself off to the camp on my bike. Sure enough, as soon as I got there I saw a gendarme standing at the entrance of the camp. I was, of course, in civilian clothes. There was no way to back out, so I pretended I had been assigned for work to a local farmer outside and was just coming back to camp. I was allowed in without any difficulty. When my comrades saw me they thought I was mad, as the gendarmes had obviously been looking for me everywhere! They urged me to leave the same night, before I was discovered and that was exactly what I did, although not without difficulties this time, because I had to negotiate my bike and myself in Indian-Sioux belly-fashion through the wire surrounding the camp without being observed! It was the last time that I saw my comrades who were kept in the camp until the Germans arrived; many were later sent to concentration camps and died at German hands.

Among my many good friends, with most of whom I had been together for almost two years, there was Jacques Offenbacher, one of our cooks, who later settled in Montauban and then in New York; our Camp Doctor, Philippson, who also settled in Montauban; Gerd Wollheim, who became a well-known expressionist painter in New York; Max Schindler, who later lived in Toulouse; Frank, our postal clerk, a mere boy at the time, who went to Switzerland; Edelstein, who worked in the sick-bay; Pelikant and Breuer and Abbott, all of whom survived the war, I am told.

The tragedy was that so many could not save themselves, among them Pechmann, Jeremias and Hirsch and so many others whose faces I can recall so perfectly but whose names I have forgotten. I have dedicated this book to their memory.

When my farmer friends brought breakfast to me in bed the following morning they found me there as usual. Had they known where I had been that night they would, rightly, have called me an imbecile!

The intelligence I had gathered made it imperative for me to leave within the next few days and to proceed to another hide-out, which I had prepared further away from the camp.

It would have been very mean of me to have left my benefactors without telling them and thanking them for their hospitality and the risk they had taken. I knew I could trust them implicitly. There was, of course, no question of paying them anything so I gave my golden cufflinks to the farmer, but I had nothing for his wife.

Two nights later, at 2 o'clock in the morning, I set out again on my bike and cycled the odd thirty kilometres to "Old Marguerite's" farmhouse near Montauban, where nobody was surprised at my arrival in the middle of the night.

"Old Marguerite" must have been on the wrong side of eighty when I first got to know her. A real character, a survivor if ever there was one, with a heart of gold and enough common sense for all her protegés. The word money was unknown to her and she never asked for gratitude.

There were four of us hiding under her roof, not all of them on the same level; those most in danger, like myself, slept in the hayloft and at first we were fed there too. Thinking back now, I remember vividly how harmonious our days were, with never a quarrel or a raised voice from any of us, and I cannot remember a single day of boredom, even though we could not leave the house, which was one of the few having survived the great floods in the Montauban area in the thirties.

First to arrive at Marguerite's was Knut, an old school pal of mine, the only one who was actually not hiding, as his health had been too poor to be conscripted into the Prestataire service. His papers were in order and it was actually through him that I got to know "Old Marguerite", who simply adored him! At that time Knut was already suffering from an incurable illness which greatly affected his mobility and from which he later died at an early age. He was one of those rare characters who never complain and who are more interested in other people than themselves. A wonderful companion, especially in difficult times. He was the first to leave for Spain, even before the Germans arrived in the unoccupied zone of France and I was very fortunate to meet him again in Madrid and later in London, where I arrived before him and from where he eventually emigrated to the United States.

The second was Michael Werner, another old friend. Michael never got conscripted into the "Prestataires", as his wife Josette was a citizen of Luxembourg. They had rented a flat in Montauban where I often spent my free time, a great relief for me from the awful conditions in Camp Septfond!

As the situation for Jews in Vichy France became more difficult in the autumn of 1942, Michael thought it more prudent to go into hiding and took refuge with "Old Marguerite".

Meanwhile, Josette who stayed on in the flat, made arrangements for both of them to cross the mountains into Spain. Michael was the second to leave our hiding place and he and his wife reached Madrid after some tribulations. More of them later.

Then there was Lucie, also a dear old friend of mine, from my years in Paris before the war, very reliable, but not adaptable. I shall never forget the one occasion when we were both alone in the farmhouse. The others had already left by then and "Old Marguerite" had gone to see her neighbour. Suddenly, French Vichy Police swarmed into the farmyard, their vehicles screeching to a halt, just leaving us time to rush to the loft, where dry beans were stored in large amounts. "Let's make love, for heaven's sake" I whispered, "that is the only thing the French respect and they will not bother us." Being rather a prude, Lucie refused to live up to the situation; fortunately the Vichy Police never came up to our loft, as just when they were about to continue their search, "Old Marguerite" came back with a broad "Bonjour Messieurs". She did not even query their presence in her house, and when they saw her simple peasant face, they could not imagine that she was capable of hiding anything, let alone Jewish refugees! Lucie never made it to Spain, but managed to survive in France. She later came to see us quite often in London, but her refusal in the hayloft, which might have cost us our lives, was never mentioned again!

As for "Old Marguerite" who once again, by her presence of mind, must have saved our lives, I often tried to imagine how she was able to take this invasion of foreigners so easily into her stride and apparently enjoy it, when she was only used to the invasion of chickens and ducks into her living room! This, of course, continued whilst we were there and with her two cats who constantly made off with her meagre meat ration before she had a chance to even consider whether to boil or fry it. She really had a full house!

Another wonderful thing about staying with her was that she lived without fear of what the next day would bring, and thus had a very calming influence on us. Of course she took great risks hiding us, but I do not think that she ever gave this a thought!

At night we used to sit in front of her fireplace in the living room, with its stone floor and its inner walls just as rough as the outer ones. I can still smell the wood, mainly gathered by her, briskly burning under a huge kettle suspended above it. That was also the way she cooked all her food, in a pot suspended above the open fire. She seemed to be busy with one thing and another all day, never resting, and I believe she therefore welcomed our evenings of relaxation in front of the fire. I have often thought since, how in centuries gone by hunting noblemen sometimes had a meal given to them by a poor farmer, whom they later rewarded with fabulous gifts and I wished I could have done this with "Old Marguerite", but I was neither nobleman nor hunter, just the hunted! Once again I was given proof of how wonderfully ordinary French people behaved individually.

My parents of course, still believed me to be in the Camp Septfonds and merrily wrote to that place, only to have their letters returned with the remark that I had left without leaving an address. I could not write to them under my own name nor did I want any of their letters to reach my hiding place, especially with an English stamp on it.

I have since found some of the letters I wrote from my hide-out signed with a pseudonym. In them I said that the doctor wanted me to spend some time in the countryside because of my poor health and that I was even thinking of paying a visit to a certain friend whose name, as she lived in Switzerland, would convey to my parents that I was playing with the idea of fleeing there, if I could. On the other hand, I said that I would rather like to join my sister, who of course was in England! The letters were a cry for help, as I had no idea what would happen to me if my plans of reaching England were not to succeed.

These were extraordinary times, and despite our day-to-day existence, our minds were constantly occupied with the future and our main thought was "how to get to England". Although the atmosphere could at times be described as balmy during the last days of what was then the "Free Zone" of France where Germans were hardly ever seen, it was clear to all of us that this would soon change and that we would have to do something about shifting ourselves towards Spain and the Pyrenees, the recognised escape route. Not much was known about what would happen on the other side, indeed not much was known about the Pyrenees and how one was to cross them. Nevertheless, one thing was clear, once the Germans had occupied the whole of France, there could be little hope of hiding forever or managing to escape.

I did not have to wait long. I vividly remember the morning of November 8th 1942, when our neighbour, Monsieur Kitrosser, a journalist from the French magazine "Match", stormed into the communal living-room shared by us and nearly all the animals in the farmyard, and gave us the news that the Allies had landed in North Africa. I can still see him now, as he blotted out the light standing in the frame of the door with his 23-stone body in a snow-white suit which the Vichy Police had only recently chased through the golden cornfield outside, arresting him for being Jewish and foreign, but bringing him back later because being a White Russian he was not yet on their lists.

He and his charming wife had rented the house together with another White Russian couple, Alexander and Eugenie Hodjack. They were the only other foreigners for miles around and we often went to their house for "Ersatz" coffee and sometimes even real coffee and often some unexpected culinary surprise. Kitrosser had also been in Septfond with me and had been released on medical grounds. Before he left the camp he asked the Commandant, Capitaine Prévot, whether he could take some pictures and was granted permission. In fact, he secretly took two sets, one as it really was in all its squalor and one which he could submit to Capitaine Prévot for his approval, some of which are reproduced in this book.

I found the Kitrossers and Hodjacks wonderful company and I am glad to say that we continued being friends when I visited them in Paris after the war.

Anyhow, this was the signal to start packing, as the Germans would not be long now in occupying the entire country.

Twenty four hours later we could see German armoured vehicles passing the farmyard at speed, frightening our hens and ducks even more than us.

High time to leave before they got organised along the Spanish border.

"Come on Lucie," I said to my companion, "Pack your bags, we are going over the mountains!"

"Not I, thank you."

I then realised we had never discussed this possibility seriously. I took it for granted she would join me. However, nothing could persuade her.

It was not easy to say goodbye to Lucie and especially "Old Marguerite", who had been host to us during the last few weeks, feeding all of us on her one ration card with the help of lots of home-grown tomatoes and corn, which she grew in profusion to feed her ducks.

She was horrified when we told her we also eat corn. In France, she would say, we only feed them to livestock. We were quite happy to be livestock and add corn to our meagre diet.

However, on the night of my departure we had a rare feast when our host dipped into her precious reserve of ducks, preserved in splendid earthenware jugs just for such an occasion.

Thus finished another chapter in my life.

CHAPTER
NINE

The following morning I left Montauban on my way south towards Spain, and I now take up the narrative again where I broke off.

You will remember the gourd-maker's promise to give me a signal at 9 o'clock that evening in the bar of the hotel in Burg-Madame, by using his handkerchief, whereupon I was to follow him outside and meet my guide.

I did not know what to do about my hotel bill. If I paid it and was then seen leaving the hotel at night, this might arouse suspicion; on the other hand I could not bring myself to leave without paying. Then an idea came to me and I paid for two nights, saying that I would have to leave early on the second morning. Nobody would query this and it would therefore not look suspicious if I went out after the gourd-maker had given me the arranged sign in the bar that same evening. As I was not allowed to take even a small parcel with me, I decided to put on double clothing of everything from shirt to socks, a decision I later bitterly regretted when during the one-and-a-half hour "cross-country-obstacle-race" — the only way to describe the border crossing — I became so overheated that I had to shed all surplus garments.

It was evening by now and close to the arranged time for the signal. I entered the bar at the very last moment, afraid that someone may talk to me and delay my departure when the signal would be given. The bar was busy and full of German military, but to my great relief I immediately spotted the gourd-maker near the exit. I just had time to down a "demi-blonde", which to French pub-crawlers is the equivalent of half-a-pint of beer, when my Spaniard took a large handkerchief from his pocket and blew his nose. Although I have now no recollection of it, surely this action must have increased my pulse rate at the time! Soon afterwards, I was following him outside to a cluster of trees where I found the man with the glowing cigarette, as promised.

The other Spaniard who was to cross with me, stood next to him and when I drew level we moved off without a word being spoken. I looked at the gourd-maker, but he strode on in the direction of the village, without looking back at us.

The most important moment for which I had prepared myself mentally and physically as much as I could, had finally arrived. My whole life was now hinged on the question "will we make it without being spotted?" I fully believed in the integrity of our guide which seemed to me beyond doubt. However, I had always heard that one had to cross the Pyrenees to get into Spain, but had never thought of walking through them at ground level, so to speak, which I understood was now his intention. My two companions were much taller and I got the feeling right from the start that I would have to catch up with them most of the time. The mere thought of it left me breathless and I started sweating underneath my multiple clothing. We had begun to walk if one could call it that. It was a dark and moonless night; our clothes were dark and I was trying hard not to lose sight of my companions. An invisible force propelled me forward, but the steering was not in my hands.

The next ninety minutes were sheer hell and much as I tried to keep pace with the guide and the other man, they constantly had to wait for me. I described it before as a "cross-country obstacle-run" and that is exactly what it was, but "at the double". I remember mainly fences and brooks which we constantly had to negotiate and then the forest-bracken, which gave us a lot of trouble. I was forced to discard most of my duplicate outfits to increase my mobility, ashamed of the fact that the other two had always to wait for me when speed was the essence, since the less time we spent crossing the border, the less chance there was that we would be spotted! Nothing lasts for ever and just as I was about to give up in despair, I saw the outlines of a large farmhouse. Unless we had run in a circle, we should by now be in Spain, I concluded. Just then my guide, obviously glad himself that my ordeal would soon be over, gave me the encouraging news that we had arrived.

As we were approaching, a man came running towards us and before I knew what was happening I saw my young Spanish travel companion fly into his arms. He had met his father at last after a long absence.

Soon we were all inside the Spaniard's house with the door safely locked behind us. Now it was my turn to be greeted — not by my father, alas, but by the three beautiful daughters of my absent host, who had already prepared a fantastic meal for us. I simply could not believe it! Was I dreaming or hallucinating like those wanderers in the desert spotting an oasis on the horizon, when there is none? I had to pinch myself.

This was the fourth year of the war and, apart from the short period I was hiding in farmhouses in France, I hadn't stayed in a proper house since it all began.

One of the lovely girls who spoke French asked me to take my shoes and socks off. I had visions of the French camp when they took our shoes away before the arrival of the Germans! Was that done again to prevent me from leaving? My anxiety was shortlived when the girl arrived with a large bowl of water and started to wash my feet. I have never forgotten this symbolic gesture; my feet were neither swollen nor dirty, but it was the thought behind this gesture which deeply touched me.

I was anticipating at best, to sleep on the floor that night and was very surprised when I was shown to a most comfortable room and bed. It was sheer bliss! Little did I know then that this was to be my last night in comfort and freedom for a long time to come!

CHAPTER
TEN

The following morning I was told that I would be put on the train to Barcelona that very day. It was clear to me that the house where we had been given such splendid hospitality, was well within the fifty kilometres safe distance from the border, and that my hosts wanted me to be fifty kilometres away from France as soon as possible, so that I would no longer be in danger of being sent back, which was the rule at that time. I did not allow myself even to contemplate the idea of being caught so near the border, but I was anxiously enquiring what would happen if I were caught further inland. The answer was that I would be sent to the British Consul in Barcelona, which I believed, but unfortunately this was not what actually happened.

Having taken my leave of the Spaniard's family, after thanking them profusely for their hospitality, given to us with complete disregard as to their personal safety, we made our way to the nearest station, the name of which I cannot remember now. This was the moment for me to split up from my companion and his father whom I was told I was "not to know" — and henceforth, I was on my own! Having been provided with a ticket, I boarded the train for Barcelona. The date was now November 15th 1942. Trying to make myself as inconspicuous as possible, in case there were police or Guardia Civil on the train, I took up position at the end of the last carriage, from where I could see the rails putting more and more kilometres between me and France.

When the train stopped for the first time, I was certain we were now fifty kilometres from the border, and I started to relax.

We were just beginning to move again when two men jumped onto the running-board, opened the door and came in. I thought to myself "lucky, they just made it" and moved out of the way to let them through.

Suddenly one of them waved an identification card at me and called out "documentacíon", which even I understood to mean that he wanted to see my papers! I had purposely left my false French identity card behind, as it would have been an easy return ticket! Now for all purposes I was English, but still without papers, which I tried to explain as best I could. "Venga con migo", "come with me", was the only answer I got and I was placed in the custody of some Guardia Civil on the train, who were already escorting another party of "Canadians" without a word of English. These were obviously Frenchmen who had also entered Spain without documents, and who were soon afterwards leaving the train with their guards on their way to Gerona.

However, one of the guards was detailed to stay with me until we reached Barcelona. By that time I still felt very confident I would be received by the British

Consul that evening to be congratulated on my escape from Occupied France! Soon the train was pulling into the station and my guard was making impatient signs for me to move. He made straight for the police post in the station where our arrival caused no stir. When I asked to be sent to the British Consulate, my demand was enthusiastically acclaimed and soon I found myself marching through the busy streets of Barcelona with an escort in front and another at the rear, both with fixed bayonets. I was just wondering how much further the Consulate could be, and what the Consul would think seeing me arriving under armed escort, when we stopped at a large building. This I was soon to find out was Police Headquarters, where on arrival I declared that my guards must have misunderstood their instructions, as I was to see the British Consul!

I began to realize that I was not making much headway when I suddenly found myself in a cell with fifteen others. I had to adjust my eyes to the little light there was and it soon dawned on me that not all inhabitants could possibly sit down at once, let alone sleep in that cell, meant for no more than six. I wondered who all these people could possibly be. Were they thieves, forgers, burglars or even worse, murderers? They did not really look the part to me. As it turned out, all of them had, just like me, come over the "green border" in the last couple of days.

I could not believe my eyes when suddenly a young lady, dressed like a waitress, appeared with a menu and I, being a late-comer — the others had already eaten — was given a very good meal carried in from a nearby restaurant. I found out from the others that the "American Joint Distribution Committee" was providing this for all illegal immigrants at Police Headquarters!

Having thought myself the only one who escaped from France that day, I was very downcast to observe that it was quite a common occurrence and that all my cell-mates had done the same thing, most of them under much more difficult conditions, as they had come over the mountains and not as I did, through the valley.

Nothing much else happened that night and I remember spending most of it standing up with occasional sit-downs on the floor. This regime with meals from outside continued for some three days, but came abruptly to an end when we were transferred to the famous Barcelona jail "Carcel Modelo".

CHAPTER
ELEVEN

On arrival we were asked for our names and religion. When I said "ebraico", which is the Spanish word for Hebrew, the prison officials laughed heartily, took it for a great joke and entered "catolico" on the admission sheet. Nothing could persuade them that I was not catholic; probably there had not been a Jew there since the Inquisition! Then we moved on to have our pockets emptied. There was little to empty in my case, except for a 500 French franc note which I had kept and which they kept now.

This note followed me to England, as one day many months later in London I received a notification from the Secretary of State of the Foreign Office, stating that a letter had been received from the Governor of Gibraltar, purporting to contain a sum of money for me and would I be good enough to come and get it. As I was by then serving in the British Army, I asked for the envelope to be forwarded to me. When I opened it, there was my original 500 franc note, forwarded by the prison authorities all the way to the Foreign Office via the Governor of Gibraltar! I really had to admire the honesty of the Spaniards and the trouble they had taken to let me have my money back. To this day I do not know how the Foreign Office managed to find me. But back to my admission at the "Carcel Modelo".

After emptying our pockets we were asked to strip and our clothes were sent for disinfection whilst we were ourselves showered and disinfected. I hardly recognised my outer garments in the heap which came back from the disinfection drums, they were so crumpled! Next visit was to the Barber's shop, not for a face-shave though, but a head-shave. Quick thinking was essential! We had, meanwhile, been given some prison-money for the pesetas we came in with and I quickly slipped five pesetas between my poor head and the blade. The result was a crew cut a quarter of an inch long which looked a lot better than the shaved heads I saw around me.

Finally we were conducted to our cell. Eight of us to share it with no beds or any other furniture, just the concrete floor and one blanket.

There was no glass in the window, high up near the ceiling, and the nights were bitterly cold. An unscreened lavatory and a washbasin, with a cold water tap, to serve all eight of us was the only other standard equipment, apart from a naked bulb and our eating utensils. No more meals from outside here, just strict prison food.

We inmates, of various nationalities, got on well with one another, respecting our privacy when performing our various bodily functions as much as this was possible under the circumstances. In fact, I cannot recall a single quarrel, although time was hanging heavily upon us, with nothing to do and no books to read or radio to listen to. There must be a certain routine in all prisons and there certainly was in the Carcel Modelo, but when one has nothing to do, every opening of the cell door seems something to look forward to, whether it is food, the man from the prison canteen or someone to call you for disinfecting.

Actually, cleanliness is one of the most important things in these conditions and I remember washing myself in cold water from head to toe every morning, and the detachable collar of my shirt every night. Once a day all prisoners were herded together in one part of the prison for the playing of the National Anthem. We had some difficult moments, as all foreigners refused to lift their arms in the fascist salute, and although the guards tried their best to make us conform, they found our arms rather limp. In the end they just gave up, although we were for some time harangued by a superior officer who lectured us about the impoliteness we were displaying by not saluting.

I remember one problem we had was shaving, as all razors were confiscated on arrival. This was overcome when one day, I climbed up to the cell window, and a Spanish prisoner in the courtyard asked us whether we wanted to buy anything and we managed to get a safety razor through him which then served us all. In fact, I kept it, having paid for it and it is still in my possession.

My cell-mates, mostly pure French, passed themselves off as Canadians — from the French speaking part of Canada, of course, — as they could hardly speak any English. They regarded me as the only genuine

Englishman in the place, a thought which I cherished and encouraged by speaking English in my sleep!

One day a consular official came to see us from the British Consulate in Barcelona. I believe that his main object was to find out whether we were really British and Canadian or just pretending to be. I asked him to let my parents in England know that I was safe and well in Spain so that they would not have to worry any longer. He never sent the message, though it would have been so easy to save them the continuing anxiety of not knowing where I was and what had happened to me. For obvious reasons I was not able to let them know where I was heading for when I left my hiding place in France, although, as I have now discovered, I had written several letters from there, signing them with my grandmother's maiden name which was Alexander. In them I had told my parents that the doctor had ordered me to stay in the country for a while on account of my poor health and that he thought it best if I came to stay with them; this was another hint that I was trying to reach England. When they eventually received my letters they understood at once, but by then I had vanished and was lost to them. I often wondered since what they would have thought if the Consulate had told them that I was "resident" at the Carcel Modelo in Barcelona!

I cannot remember exactly how long we stayed there, but it must have been something like seven weeks until we were once again moved on. During this time, although we had many deprivations and physical discomfort, none of us bore a grudge against Spain for

75

having put us in prison without a charge or any judicial proceedings. After all, we were illegal immigrants, having come over the "green border", and we were grateful that we were not sent back to France! Neither during my time did I hear any disrespectful remarks about the Allies or any praise for the Germans. In fact, among the Spanish political prisoners there seemed to be little doubt that the Allies would win in the end and we were implored to do something about them as soon as we returned to England and victory was achieved. As it turned out, they had to wait much longer than that for their liberty.

One morning in early January 1943 we were told to get ready — there was of course nothing to pack and we were driven to the station where we boarded a most uncomfortable train. It was impossible to find out its destination until many hours had passed; rumours were naturally rife. One of them was that we were on our way to Irun, the frontier with France. But why, we argued would they send us all the way to the west when we could have been sent north from Barcelona, if they really wanted to deport us. Frantic discussions ensued. Should we jump off, even if we endangered our lives or just sit it out? Although the rifles of our guards seemed a little antiquated, we were certain they would be able to use them. Fortunately, none of them understood English or for that matter French, and our discussions were quite open. In the end we decided to question our guards as to the reason for our going in a westerly direction, and found that Irun really was our destination, but what for, none of us detected. As it turned out, and we could hardly believe it when it happened, at Irun we were simply put through the formalities to legalise our entry into Spain, filling out a form and having it stamped!

The relief of it could be seen on all our faces and nobody minded when we re-embarked on the train which had waited for us. What was our destination now? Nobody knew until we got there! "Miranda de Ebro", a large Spanish internment camp for foreigners. So we had been legally accepted into Spain in order to be incarcerated once again. Some logic!

CHAPTER
TWELVE

Miranda was the place where the Spanish put the exhausted hordes who, with help from the local guides had bravely climbed over the Pyrenees escaping from the Germans, now in command of all France.

There were French, pretending to be French-speaking Canadians, Austrian and German Jews, like myself, pretending to be British, and the Poles, wanting to be nothing but Polish. To the Spaniards we were all the same.

Internment camps are not know for their comfort and Miranda was no exception. Inmates were crowded in the barracks, but had individual bunks. These were in groups of four and by hanging blankets or other material between each group of bunks and also in front of them, individual "rooms" were created which allowed a certain amount of privacy. This shut out most of the light and "lamps" which consisted of a wick dipped in olive oil were not only used for light, but also for heating water to make coffee.

There was little money about in the camp, at that time. We were paid 15 pesetas a month by the Spanish Authorities, which bought hardly anything and the "American Joint Distribution Committee", which was supposed to look after us, had apparently run out of money during that particular period, or so we were informed. Thus I missed out on January and February contributions and there were no parcels arriving either.

Everything within the camp was traded or swapped, most of the goods came from parcels received by individuals from their Embassies, the Joint Committee or the Red Cross. Visitors from other groups of bunks were always welcome and many times one could see up to twenty legs dangling from the four bunks, whilst the smell of Nescafe, provided by the host, pervaded the immediate vicinity. Water was a great problem because there were only two taps for the entire camp and queues formed early in the morning and throughout the day. There was, of course, no point queueing for just one mug of shaving water and the acquisition of a large tin or of an empty olive oil container was number one priority, and until such luxury could be obtained one just had to rely on others for some water; such favours were normally obtained by taking over duties from them, mainly peeling potatoes. Please do not think that peeling potatoes for 2,500 inmates is an easy matter when it is done by hand; it took most of the day and our hands looked and felt absolutely awful at the end. I always remember a man who owned a fish-and-chip shop where he came from, who would under no circumstances sink to such a low level as to peel potatoes, so he had to buy his way out when his turn came, but when there were no takers, which sometimes happened if there was plenty of food and some money about, he would rather have his hair cut off by the Spaniards, which was their usual way of punishment, than to submit to the indignity of peeling potatoes.

The Army was in charge of the camp and left us much to our own devices, as long as we appeared for the "Apello" when everyone was counted and the flag hoisted or lowered to the tune of the National Anthem blaring out from the loudspeakers. At night one could hear the guards shouting "ALERTA" from their watchtowers so as to indicate to their comrades and probably to themselves that they were not asleep. There was never any incident during my time and nobody tried to escape, as everyone was hoping for a quick release. However, quick release did not come and when I arrived in January 1943 the entire camp had decided to go on a hunger-strike in protest.

About 2,500 men of many nationalities were there at that time, most of them having escaped from German-Occupied France on their own initiative, and some who had missed their connection on the organised escape runs and who, like all of us, had been picked up by the Spaniards. The Polish contingent, although small, dominated the camp. Where they actually came from originally, I was never able to find out for certain, but many must have been part of the Free Polish Forces in France, others must have lived there as civilians. The hunger strike was to last seven days. The main reason for it was that the Allied authorities, who were obliged to repatriate their nationals from neutral territory or to reunite them with their units if they had been in the Forces, dragged their feet and not a single man had been released from the camp.

With hindsight I can now see that the Allies were busy with more important things at that time, than to check the credentials of the many inmates claiming to be either Canadians, Australians, British and so on, even if there were some genuine British subjects in the camp; nevertheless, those who had been in Miranda for some time felt very neglected and useless, especially as most of us were young.

As the hunger-strike continued, the entire camp while gradually getting weaker, had at first to parade for all meals which were always served in the open from enormous cauldrons. The contents were usually the same, a vegetable-and-meat brew with a lot of liquid and a generous amount of olive oil floating on it.

The first few days the cauldrons kept coming and their smell entering our nostrils made us even more hungry than we were already. Finally, the Spaniards gave up serving it. Nobody broke the strike and had anyone dared, he would no doubt have been attacked. Inmates who had been there for some time had stores left from the parcels they had received earlier and no doubt nibbled at them in the privacy of their bunks; having just arrived I was not in such a fortunate position and had to see the thing through without help. One week without food seems a very short period, but I remember feeling terribly weak, especially as I had already suffered many months of deprivation. However, my main worry was to let my parents know that I was alive and well, as they now had not heard from me for several months. I managed to get a message to them, which they received to their great relief on January 24th.

Soon the Embassies in Madrid got to hear of what was happening in Miranda, and suddenly delegations started to arrive like magic. They were most concerned, listened patiently and made lots of promises which they were either unable to keep, or did not mean to keep in the first place. Embassies were not willing to recognise their apparently newly-acquired nationals.

Meanwhile I had become ill with jaundice and entered the camp hospital which contrasted vastly with conditions in the camp elsewhere. The Spanish authorities did not really mind what nationality you were or pretended to be and treated all inmates alike. Neither inmates nor the camp authorities made any demands on each other. As long as there was sufficient labour provided to prepare the food for which they were responsible, the authorities did not bother about you. On the other hand, there was no possibility to complain about the most unsatisfactory hygienic conditions in the camp, as for instance the primitive "loos" without any water whatsoever, either for cleaning up the mess of the two-and-a-half thousand inmates using it, or for washing one's hands. Without wanting to go into details, it was impossible to reach the hole in the concrete provided at the top end of the several runs between the walls which led up to the hole, without getting one's feet soiled. The only time the place ever looked clean was during the hunger strike! It was probably mainly due to the large amounts of disinfectant used that the camp escaped an epidemic disaster.

In hospital, where I now found myself, it was a different matter. You became their total responsibility and I received excellent medical attention. Medicines which were difficult to obtain, such as insulin, were given to me daily and diets were strictly observed. The hospital in the camp was clean and warm and for someone who had slept on straw or on a cement floor or, at best, on a bunk for years, a hospital bed was sheer delight, especially the clean sheets. No-one seemed to be in a hurry to throw me out until I was alright after some three weeks.

When I returned to the camp I found that things were moving at last. In the middle of March 1943, people had started to leave Miranda. More and more food parcels arrived from the various Embassies and refugee organisations and in consequence the whole food situation improved. You will remember the Spanish bride I met on the train in France. Well, I could hardly believe it when I received a lovely parcel from her family in Zaragossa with whom I had been in contact. I really was touched, as I had never met them. Soon afterwards I got a job as assistant to the Red Cross Station in the camp with the view of being trained to take over, as the person in charge, from Herbert Landsberger, who was the brother-in-law of my friend Knut, mentioned earlier, as he was leaving the camp. Incidentally it was he who introduced me to my first "Muesli", as he had got hold of some Scottish oats to which we added fruit and nuts and topped it

83

with milk and sugar obtained from the first parcels he received.

I was able to move to a much better hut, really cosy, but just as I was getting used to the "posh" surroundings, I received news that David Blickenstaff had obtained my release from Miranda.

David was Director of the "American Quakers" and the "American Joint Distribution Committee" set up in Madrid to assist all refugees not looked after by their Embassies. He later became Assistant to Trigvie Lee, the first Secretary of the United Nations. I could hardly contain myself with joy! One step nearer to my goal and England! Also the idea to be free again after such a long time of total and virtual confinement in Spain and in France, before that.

CHAPTER
THIRTEEN

The long awaited day of freedom finally arrived. Having packed my few belongings I was eagerly awaiting my liberator's arrival at the camp. I had said goodbye to all my friends and was ready to be called. The hours passed, I remember it was a hot day in May, but nothing happened. I could not stand the suspense any longer and made my way to the administrative building at the camp entrance, only to learn that David had been and gone. I felt forlorn and abandoned and wondered whether I would ever leave Miranda! What could have gone wrong? My Spanish was not really good enough to enquire; when suddenly I was handed a letter. It was from David, explaining that my release papers were not in order and that he hoped to come back for me shortly. I was much relieved, and true to his promise I was freed shortly afterwards.

I had not been in neutral territory since the beginning of World War II and so Madrid in the early summer of 1943, after all the experiences I had gone through, seemed to be almost unreal. Having come from war-torn France with the Germans constantly on ones heels, Madrid with no war, no black-out, no rationing, or danger of any kind was haven indeed!

David wanted me to work in his office, as I had previous experience in refugee work in France for Baron Robert de Rothschild before the war. My friend Knut who had been freed before me, was living in a Spanish Pension in 10 Zorilla, in the centre of Madrid, and he got me a room there which I shared with a young Spaniard, Lorenzo, a native of the Canary Islands. There were only young Spaniards of both sexes living in the pension; we were all working and came back for lunch and dinner which were hilarious affairs full of good talk and badinage. We often went out together in the evenings and I remember that several times we went to Festivals in the streets, which reminded me very much of the French National Holiday, 14th July, when all Paris dances in the streets. We used to form enormous human chains, holding hands and running all over the place. I had forgotten that life could be fun, not having had any since the beginning of the war.

I went to the office every week-day and worked hard, about nine hours a day, split by the siesta which makes the day much longer.

Anyone familiar with Spanish mealtimes will know that a day is really three days in one — the morning finishes at 2p.m., when one goes for lunch, then comes the siesta; the afternoon starts at 5 and we usually closed the office at 9; dinner is at 10 and after that the "third day" starts at 11, with theatres and cinemas starting at that time. One never goes to bed much before two in the morning when one has to shout at the top of one's voice for the "Serrano" who is holding the keys for all the houses in his area. Having attracted his attention — which might take some time when he is not nearby — he immediately found the right key and let one in for the usual tip. I found this system much preferable to the ringing of the bell for the concierge in France, to whom you have to shout out your name when you pass and who remembers how many times you came in late!

In the early summer of 1943 things at first did not look so good militarily; our mood was sombre and when we talked English we often got certain looks which were difficult to define. Was it pity or pleasure? Although I was surrounded by Spanish friends who were convinced that the Allies would win the war, one often got the impression that the man in the street was not. However, with victories in Africa later that summer things began to change. We took pleasure in reading in public to each other, either on the trams or in cafés on the sidewalks, bulletins which we received daily from the American and British Embassies. On one occasion we were sitting in a café near the Palace Hotel where a group of Germans was sitting next to us and we started reading our bulletins aloud; one could gauge from their reactions that the tide was finally turning for us.

Days in the office became more and more hectic. Refugees arrived all the time.

I had seen it all before in France in the spring and summer of 1939, when my task was much the same, with the only difference being that we all lived in the disused hotel, whose "guests" intensively trained for jobs which never materialised because of the war. Four years later in Madrid they could have been the same people, refugees once more!

Interviewing them, checking whether they were genuine, arranging for their accommodation, allocating funds for them, trying to trace their families and arranging emigration and transportation for those who were lucky enough to have affidavits to support their visa applications for the United States, (leaving by "Clipper" from Lisbon) took up most of our time. In addition to these physical, financial and emigration problems, there were of course the many human problems the staff of the "Quakers" and the "American Joint Distribution Committee", under the apt leadership of David Blickenstaff, had to deal with daily. I seem to remember that we kept on adding to our filing system, where not only all the names of the refugees passing through the office were recorded; but also all their living relatives and any person able to help, with cross references. Even every member of staff had a card and I recall David being very upset that we did not have a card for him, the boss, which was immediately rectified!

After a couple of months in Madrid I was offered a room in the flat where my friend Knut stayed, as his sister was leaving. The flat belonged to a most charming Spanish lady who provided not only the room but also all the meals. I could now go home every day for lunch, have a couple of showers in the summer heat and a most useful "siesta", which made it possible to work just as hard in the afternoon.

During my time in Madrid I made many friends, men and women. None better than Mimo who was then one of the few practising women barristers, whom I visited after the war with my wife and with whom I still maintain a lively correspondence. She and her husband, José-Luis, who sadly died some time ago, had six children, two of whom have now joined their mother in her lawyers office.

There was Mercedes, a budding actress whom I adored, very Spanish, very beautiful, very vivacious, very tall and English speaking. She used to collect me from the office. I can see her now, sitting on a nearby wall. Her long legs spread out sideways from the knees in her typical pose, wearing black stockings, which I hated. Her chestnut hair golden in the afternoon sun.

She would stand up and smile the moment she saw me, silently take my arm and lead me to our favourite café for "fresas con natta" — strawberries with whipped cream. We spent a lot of our free time together and I was proud to be seen with her in the open air places like the Retiro park, where she nearly fell into the lake on one of our boat trips. We laughed a lot. Dear Merche, as we called her, I wish I could have seen her once more, but most sadly she died in 2002.

My only consolation is that a few days before she died our mutual friend Mimo read her the short story I had written about her, recalling our youth.

There were also friends who, like me had come over from France, such as Josette and Michael Werner. Michael was, of course, with me in hiding with "Old Marguerite", but before that he and Josette were still living in Mountauban and I had often been to their room, which Josette had made into a real home for their friends, who while they were still allowed to, turned up on Sundays from the camp, which was quite a distance away. Josette, born in Luxembourg, a very good friend since our days in Vichy France, was a woman of great personality, with strong opinions which she had no fear in expressing. She came under the protection of the Luxembourg Embassy in Spain and they really looked after her! Her husband, Michael, also worked in David Blickenstaff's office. We had been together for many years and shared many memories, not all of them pleasant. Fortunately they both survived the war and I met them many times again in Paris and Grasse, where they finally settled.

All my Spanish friends were sympathetic to the Allied cause and this gave me great encouragement. Then there was Janine, David's French wife, who also worked in his office, a highly intelligent woman, sympathetic to the troubles of the refugees and a great help to her husband. I shall never forget a terribly funny episode which happened one afternoon when we both returned after a shopping expedition for some office furniture, which David needed for his office. We had acquired a beautiful coffee-table which made its first appearance in his office that same afternoon, followed soon by a visit from the American Consul. David, who believed in making everyone feel at ease and comfortable, asked him to put his feet up, which the good Consul promptly did, but unfortunately with such gusto that the poor coffee-table collapsed!

In spite of our long working hours we always found time "to live". For anyone who likes out-door life, sitting in street cafés, shaded by the green leaves of the trees, with strawberries and cream or a drink in the company of friends, Madrid is the right place. Then there was, of course, the "Prado", one of Europe's most important picture galleries housing the great Spanish masterpieces, such as Velazquez, Goya and El Greco, in particular. All this made one almost forget the war.

Although I came to realise that the work I was doing in Madrid was important, and that I was helping David in his difficult task of dealing with hundreds of war refugees in a neutral country, to which they had managed to escape, usually under the most difficult circumstances, I never lost sight of my original goal, which was to reach England and to join the Army and my family.

Meanwhile, my parents who lived in Farnham, Surrey, since they came to England just before the outbreak of war, had heard through the Red Cross, after many months without news, that I had escaped from the Germans in France and was safe in Miranda, even if I was still in a camp. Strenuous efforts were made by them to make it possible for me to continue on my journey to England, an almost hopeless undertaking it would seem, in the middle of a war.

However, this was not the way I saw it — Madrid for me, was merely a staging post! It was only after my mother's death many years later that I came across the vast amount of correspondence my parents had with the contacts they established, in particular with the then Bishop of Chichester, Dr. Bell, who had a long-standing reputation for helping refugees from the Nazis and whose assistance must have been instrumental in having my visa application at the Consulate in Madrid looked at in a favourable manner.

In the Spring of 1943, Wilfred Israel, a close friend of Dr. Bell and now well known for the tremendous work he did for Jewish refugees from Nazi oppression, especially children separated from their parents, had left London for Lisbon and Madrid in order to negotiate on their behalf with the authorities, and to investigate further possibilities to get them to safety and to find a destination for them in what was then Palestine, or in whatever country was willing to accept them. Before leaving London, Wilfred Israel had asked Dr. Bell whether he would like to name anyone he would like him to see in Spain and I was fortunate enough to be one of them. I still remember vividly the day when he came to see me in David Blickenstaff's office in Calle Edoardo Dato. Although I had never met him before — and he was not an outgoing person according to his biographers — we had immediate contact, probably in view of my work. I must have been one of the last persons to see him alive as shortly afterwards his plane, in which the famous actor Leslie Howard was also travelling, was tragically shot down by the Germans on its flight back to London from Lisbon, although it was a civilian plane. They were led to believe that Churchill was aboard, as he was due to return at that time from a visit to the North African front. There were no survivors. We were, of course, horrified, as indeed the entire world was when we came to hear about it.

CHAPTER
FOURTEEN

Unfortunately, my father had died quite suddenly in February 1943, and never knew the results of his efforts to get me to England, but at least he knew that I was alive and well. The sad news of his death had reached me belatedly during my most difficult time in Miranda, in the middle of March. The awful thing was that I had continued to write to both my parents for three weeks after my father passed away, since the tragic news of his death had not reached me. In fact, my mother's account of his funeral arrived before the letter in which she told me that he had died suddenly; so the shock to me was devastating!

It took me a very long time to get over it, especially as it was so unexpected. We had a particularly good relationship and he was more like a friend to me than a father. I still so vividly remember the long walks we had through Berlin's Tiergarten, after breakfast on the terrace of Moehring, the famous "Konditorei" on the Kurfuerstendamm, he to his office and I to mine. There was nothing that I could not discuss with him on these walks. It was he who awakened my interest in all the arts and I am eternally grateful to him for that, as I can now enjoy them so much more.

He and my mother had always been my champions. Sound advice, when needed, praise and criticism when deserved, money, whether deserved or not and which they could often ill afford after their emigration, was generously given to me during our many years of separation, which I could not have survived without their constant love and care. In fact, it is only now, some sixty years later, having read through the correspondence between us, amounting to many hundreds of letters over these years, that I came to appreciate it fully.

When I left Germany at the age of 18, after Hitler came to power in 1933, a regular weekly exchange of letters developed between us. Although I lost all their letters during the war and made no copies of mine, my parents not only kept all my letters but also made carbon copies of their letters to me between 1933 and 1943, which now makes fascinating reading, because I can recall every detail of what happened during these eventful ten years, which covered emigration when I was still in my teens, my career in the hotel industry in France and Italy, the refugee relief work I was involved in and the war years. I do not know how they ever found the time to write such long letters, full of love and advice on all subjects, and general guidelines to keep me out of trouble and to prepare me for the tough life ahead.

My most prized possession is a letter which my father wrote to me on my 21st birthday. This came back to me through most unusual circumstances, together with all the other correspondence exchanged between

1933 and 1939. My parents had sent these letters to Rotterdam in a container for storage, before they themselves sailed for England in the German liner "Europa" just three weeks before war broke out. This container, into which my parents had put all their worldly belongings, never reached England and eventually fell into German hands when Holland was occupied in May 1940, and it was never seen again, with the miraculous exception of those letters.

One day in 1961 an aunt of mine spotted a notice in the "Jerusalem Post" asking for my father's and my whereabouts. The notice had been put in by The Jewish Historical General Archives in Jerusalem. The entire bundle of correspondence between my parents and myself, which had been in this container in Rotterdam, had been sent to their office in Jerusalem by someone in Holland or elsewhere, who had found it and thought it worth the trouble to save it and to preserve it for posterity!

CHAPTER
FIFTEEN

It was not an everyday occurrence that civilians as I then was, were allowed or indeed encouraged to come to the U.K. in the middle of the war. Therefore I was of course overjoyed when one day in September 1943 a dispatch rider from the British Embassy came to our office in the Calle Eduardo Dato with my marching orders. My parents had done a great job! I knew David Blickenstaff wanted me to stay on with him and even go to Italy when it would be possible to open an office there, but he understood why I wanted to join the British Army.

All my friends in Madrid were over the moon and so was I, although I knew it would be many years before I would be able to live the life of Madrid again, even when the war was over. The friends I had made there, among both Spaniards and refugees, and of course my friend David and his family, had been good to me and the work there had greatly satisfied me. I suppose I could have been forgiven for wanting to stay there until the end of hostilities, but then I would not have been true to myself and to my original and steadfast aim throughout these long years.

In life one often waits a long time for things to happen, which one desperately wants and when they suddenly materialise there is usually an anti-climax. In this case it was not so, even though I was sad to leave so many of my new friends behind. There was not much time for goodbyes, as I had to leave the very next day for Gibraltar. On the train I was given a British passport. "Not for keeps", the man said, "Just for the frontier".

I was by now so used to peaceful Spain that the sudden plunge into the military atmosphere of Gibraltar where I arrived on the 20th September 1943 at the Spanish Pavilion, had quite a sobering effect on me, although it would not be correct to describe the atmosphere as a warlike one. It was more that of a military camp, like Aldershot, but far removed from the zone of war and without the dread of nightly air attacks. Everyone seemed to be busy preparing for the next convoy, either to arrive or to leave.

So I explored Gibraltar. First the NAFI, an organisation which I was to appreciate in the years to come. Then the Library, where I got some good books to while away the long evenings of waiting.

I had no particular task to perform whilst waiting for the convoy, which would eventually take me on board, and nothing much happened except one day when I was resting at my barracks I was given a message ordering me to report at some office. When I arrived there it turned out to be a French outfit, probably the office of some French military authority or part of the Consulate. It did not take them very long to get to the point which was that they wanted me to join their Foreign Legion. This was not the first attempt by the French to coerce me and I really had fears of being press-ganged and saw myself already being bundled on a ship going to North Africa. Fortunately, I speak French fluently and persuaded them that there was no way for me to join the Legion as I was on my way to London to join the British Army. If they did not believe it, they could get in touch with the military authorities. After that categorical statement I made my exit which was not impeded.

Soon afterwards I was told to hold myself ready for embarkation.

Young people today can not begin to realise what immense organisation was needed to assemble a convoy such as ours in times of war, which consisted of 65 ships of all sizes. They would come to the Straits of Gibraltar from many different parts and carry much needed material and food for the U.K.

When we finally embarked, I found myself one of only seven civilians aboard and I was wondering where I would fit in. Apparently someone must have thought that I was an officer and a most comfortable cabin was given to me. However, we could not have been more than twenty minutes at sea, when someone discovered that I was not an officer, and I was hastily sent down a few decks and given a hammock, just above the waterline. I had never slept in a hammock before and I found it a fascinating experience which I enjoy to this day, but where I was sleeping a torpedo could not possibly have missed me, even if it tried!

The ships of our convoy were assembling in the Straits and outside in the Atlantic. To send them all off together heading for mid-Atlantic protected by the Royal Navy was no mean task. It was fantastic to see how everything fell into place and everyone knew exactly what to do and where to go.

In peace-time it would not have taken more than four days to reach the U.K., but we had to pull out to mid-Atlantic in order to escape any German war ships or planes on the look-out for us, and consequently the voyage took twelve days in all. I had never been on any ship for so long. Mine was a cruise liner of some 14,000 tons converted for use as a troop-ship. Life on board was pleasant enough and I did not get seasick, probably because we did not have to negotiate the Bay of Biscay. The only real problem I encountered was with my soap which just would not lather in the seawater, until some kind soul put me right and gave me a piece of sea-water soap and the problem was solved instantly!

The soldiers on board did not really know what to make of me and my colleagues in civilian clothes who were sharing their quarters; they did not know who we were and what we were doing among them. I suppose I liked this air of mystery and as I managed to get along well with them, no explanations were necessary. Nowadays when you meet British people, most of them will ask you where you come from if they detect the slightest accent, and if you say "Hampstead" this will not satisfy them and produce a further query, such as "I mean originally," but in wartime things were different and not so many questions were asked.

It was not exactly a luxury-cruise, but then on the other hand, one was never bored; there were books to read, "Housy Housy" was played by all — the game which we now know as "Bingo". A lot of time was spent on deck watching the other 64 ships of the convoy around us, a unique and truly amazing sight, which never failed to fascinate me. Normally one would not see so many ships close by, all going at the speed of the smallest or slowest craft, so that it would not fall behind. Of course, this made the whole convoy very vulnerable! A mechanical breakdown in any one of the ships could arrest the whole convoy and make it a sitting duck for the Germans. Fortunately, this did not happen, but the thought was ever present.

Of course, we were not entirely undetected and on several occasions we were attacked from the air. When this happened one was conscious of a terrific noise from the attacking planes and from the ships' "ack-ack" guns. Miraculously no ships or lives were lost during any of these attacks. I was quite amazed how calm everyone remained during these dangerous moments. Nevertheless, I think the whole ships' company was glad when we finally docked in Greenock, Scotland, at the end of our long voyage.

My first reaction was an ardent desire to kiss the soil, as I had finally made it! Royal Navy establishments ashore seem to have a kind of special atmosphere which no doubt stems from the long tradition of the Senior

Service, and which makes one feel immediately at home, very much as I imagine life on board a Royal Navy vessel in peace time, visiting foreign ports. A lot of discipline, combined with the most generous hospitality, not only in terms of food and drinks but also in a desire to make certain that the Navy's guests, whether they are invited on board or are picked up after a disaster at sea, are really made welcome and looked after. The Navy did not fail us on this occasion either and welcomed us with a really splendid Scottish breakfast, porridge and all.

CHAPTER
SIXTEEN

In England

However, what I was most looking forward to — a hot bath and a change of clothes — had to wait until we reached London. The train carrying us there during the night had all blinds drawn and my desire to see the "Promised Land" had to wait until dawn broke the following morning. I could not take my eyes off the lush greens and the beautiful peaceful countryside. Now I could understand for the first time what my parents meant when they described the beauties of England again and again in their letters to me. One could hardly believe that the country was in its fourth year of war!

I knew that London had gone through the "Blitz" and the "Battle of Britain" and my first impression on my arrival in the middle of October 1943 was one of surprise that so much was still standing and how normal life seemed to be. Of course, many men and women in the street were in uniform and there were a lot of sandbags propped up against buildings and windows bricked up and other buildings had come down. Nevertheless, the general impression I got from the start was that here was a City which had come to terms with the situation and was determined to lick

103

Hitler, cost what may, whilst trying to preserve the quality of life as much as it was possible under the circumstances, whether through the arts — and here I remember most vividly the lunchtime concerts — or by the help, encouragement and comradeship its inhabitants gave each other.

On arrival in London we civilians were taken to another Reception Centre, the "Patriotic School" in Wandsworth, for screening before we were let loose on the streets of London. There we were held "incommunicado" for about two weeks. Somehow, I look back with great pleasure to the period I spent there. I could not exactly say why, probably because I was so happy that I had finally "made it" to England. The two weeks passed very quickly. Suddenly, on November 2nd 1943, a sergeant collects me with an army vehicle the size of a tank, and tyres larger than those of a bus. Where are we going? I am finally being drafted. Enrolled in the Territorial Army, sworn in by Major A.J. Blake at No.3 Recruiting Centre in Tottenham Court Road. I had finally achieved what I had set out to do!

I do not understand to this day how I passed as "A1" and remained so throughout my military life, because I am almost blind without my glasses, otherwise I seem to have been all right, but my glasses struck me as a great handicap at the time. Finally I found myself in the streets of London, a free man at last! My only desire now was to serve and in my small way to help to bring this war to the desired conclusion.

Throughout my voyage to England I had been thinking of being reunited with my mother and sister at long last. Now that I had passed all the hurdles which had seemed insurmountable when I first planned this journey many months ago in Occupied France and I had finally achieved my aim to join the British Army, my next thought was for them. I was wondering how much time the Army would give me to see them. I did not have to wait long for the answer, it was exactly three days. They seemed to be in a deuce of a hurry to get my services! Nevertheless, I was grateful when I received a leave-and-rail pass to Farnham in Surrey, where my mother still lived and which I came to love more and more over the years.

Although I had by then been in England for more than two weeks I had not been able to speak to my mother and, of course, we had never spoken to each other since the beginning of the war. So it was a great moment for both of us when I got through to her and I shall never forget the joy in her voice. As I only had three days to spend with her and my sister who was staying there on leave, I made my way to Waterloo Station straight away and took the first train to Farnham.

I had not seen my mother since 1935 and we were now in 1943!

I shall always remember the moment I stepped out of my carriage and saw my mother and sister standing at the end of the platform. The train which carried me from Waterloo to Farnham had been the last link in a long chain of events which transported me from

Occupied France to England in the middle of a war. It had taken me exactly eleven months. My long "Journey into Freedom" had come to an end and a new beginning.

CHAPTER
SEVENTEEN

I had received my marching orders before I went on leave. I was to go to Manchester and then proceed to Buxton in Derbyshire. As I was travelling up, I kept wondering what it would be like when I got there and what sort of outfit it would be. I had been given a rail-pass and my mother had provided me with enough food to last me for a week in case Army food would be insufficient! All refugees were at that time assigned to the Pioneer Corps which later — maybe in view of our good work — became the "Royal Pioneer Corps". I knew whatever was in store for me would be better than anything I had experienced in Europe, with the exception of Madrid, and I was highly pleased that finally I would be able to "do my bit" for the war effort and was prepared for anything. What I was not prepared for was Buxton.

I was absolutely enchanted with it and its beautiful countryside. I had imagined a garrison town and instead I came to a lovely old-fashioned "spa" with afternoon tea dances in the Pavilion at weekends, lovely flower arrangements in the public parks, beautiful shops and a balmy atmosphere; one certainly would not have known that there was a war on and that in one part of Buxton I was being taught the martial arts by a very conscientious and eager sergeant, typically English! We were a mixed bunch, ten percent aliens, but he would never let us aliens feel this or make any nasty remarks. I immediately liked him for his tact and fairness and the way he went about his rather difficult task. Not everyone of us was at recruiting age, I was 29, and some were older and he needed a lot of patience. Fortunately, he stayed with us all day and I was amazed to observe him as much at ease at conducting a debate, when he divided the room into two camps by saying "you lot are for the motion and you over there against it," as he was when he taught us how to run an enemy through with a bayonet. We took all of this very seriously because we knew the war was not over by a long shot, and a time might come when the knowledge acquired in peaceful Buxton might come in handy.

Our training was to take three months. During this time I enjoyed myself a great deal, so much so that I received a disapproving letter from my mother. My letters to her were full of hedonism and in her opinion I should use my spare time to further myself. With hindsight I knew she was right to reprimand me, which in any case she only did after thinking a long time about it and apologising profusely for doing so; after all if she would not tell me, no one else would. I tried to put her mind at ease, but found it extremely difficult to follow her advice at that time, which was probably my reaction to the many years when I could not take it easy, as also in Spain I had to work very hard indeed.

There was for instance Eileen — a doctor whom I met at a dance — with whom I spent a lot of time; she even came down to visit me when I was on leave at my mother's place in Farnham, where she put her feet on the mantelpiece which made my mother declare that she was no lady! Perhaps not, but she was great fun and being a doctor she had a car, which impressed my fellow Pioneers no end.

We were stationed in Lismore Camp, which was part of the Empire Hotel. My companions were not the most inspiring bunch, mainly enlisted on account of the war and I found it difficult to make friends. Hence my sorties into beautiful Buxton after duty. Life was much more pleasant and easy during this training period than at any time after that. Our laundry was washed by the Army and socks mended by the WVS — also to become "Royal" later, probably on account of all the help they extended to the Forces during the war. The Army organised concerts and dances. There was nothing unusual in having three orchestras performing at one concert in the Playhouse:- a military band, a jazz band with 13 members (five of them Saxophones) and a chamber orchestra. Then there were plays and the cinema and afternoon tea at Miller's in Main Street.

But, of course, it was not all play. Military training was very intensive and besides the usual drill, for which a sergeant and corporal were assigned to each ten recruits, we had to learn the names of all the parts of all the guns and rifles used at that time, fire them, clean them, learn how to use hand grenades, judge the wind and calculate how much a bullet would be deflected from its target and a great many other things. Little did I know then that I would have to learn the names of all the German weaponry in the Intelligence Corps, later.

I was most surprised when I found out that I could his bulls-eyes with my rifle and land my grenade right bang on target, and wondered if perhaps they were correct in classifying me "A1" in spite of my bad eyesight!

I was very sorry when my time in Buxton came to an end in the middle of February 1944 and I was posted to the "69 Company Pioneers" which was in Darlington, Co Durham, at that time. Eileen was in tears and I, a soppy soldier, was not far from them!

In Darlington we were billeted in a Hall in the centre. Our Commanding Officer had some peculiar ideas and insisted on our patrolling the peaceful streets with rifles, and wearing steel helmets. The citizens of Darlington wondered what we were about as they had never seen such a thing before, and had they questioned us we would have not been able to tell them. I reflected on how much a uniform can influence people because, quite frankly, some of the Pioneers looked very German indeed!

Another of his ideas was to keep us mobile, so one night at 3 o'clock in the morning we received orders to pack and move within 15 minutes; we marched the remainder of the night only to find ourselves back in our old Hall for breakfast! Although the Major was considered rather eccentric, he was popular with the men because he moved a lot among us and frequently spoke to us.

After a while, we left various items behind, as we were always convinced we would be back for breakfast. However, in early March this did not help us very much when one night we really marched to another destination, and I, for one, had to buy a new razor outfit and washbag.

The new destination was Sledmere in Yorkshire, where we found ourselves under canvas in the middle of some icy field covered in snow without any form of heating and one frozen water tap for all of us. How could one shave with frozen water? I remember burning hundreds of matches in order to coax a little water from that tap whilst the wind made my bristles stand on edge; fortunately, I developed the art of shaving with a thimble-full of water after having tried to store some in a bottle which exploded when the water froze! During the day we were sent to free the roads of snow and ice for the forthcoming invasion, as we were told. I thought to myself, surely they are not going to invade the Continent from Yorkshire, neither will anyone come to invade us here and concluded that it simply was the Yorkshire Country Council's idea for having their roads cleared cheaply.

After one week I decided that I had had enough of this lark and started to comb the district for a room of my own. I knocked at many doors without success; I was just about to give up and settle for my icy tent when I called at a newsagents' who had a most delightful room to let for five shillings a week, one minute from the camp. I just could not resist, I even had my own sitting room with a fireplace. From then on I could have stayed in Sledmere for ever, especially as hot water for shaving was brought up to me every morning with my newspaper. What luxury! Of course, I had to keep it a secret, as my superior officers would not have taken very kindly to my living in luxury whilst they still slept under canvas. As I appeared punctually for breakfast every morning and my other tent-dwellers having been sworn to secrecy, the whole thing worked very well.

Eileen came to visit me one day; she had announced her impending visit on the telephone last time I had rung her from the village call-box. I was much looking forward to this and the room would be much cosier than having to face the blizzards outside! Our friendship in Buxton had been platonic and I was hoping to change things, but this being 1943, and Eileen catholic and Irish, there was not a chance. I think she must have felt that I was disappointed and she had a hard time not to succumb to her feelings. In spite of our mutual disappointment I shall always remember her with fondness.

Whilst still in training I had made an application to join the Intelligence Corps. Now, more than ever, I was hoping that my talents would soon be diverted into the right channels! But, meanwhile, my Company was sent to Selby every day where coal had to be loaded by us on wagons because of a strike. Three of us managed to load 15 tons a day, which was rather exhausting because it had to be done without any mechanical help, simply with a shovel. That went on for days. Fortunately, we were under the command of an officer,

Capt. Paul Alexander, son of a Berlin Professor, who understood how to handle his men and did not mind getting his hands dirty on the job. In consequence, he was extremely popular with every man, especially as he was so approachable that one could discuss anything with him. We considered him great fun, full of humour and always trying hard to improve our lot.

After such back-breaking work it was always heaven to return to Miss Cooper's rooms, where the open fire and sometimes a cake which she had baked, would wait for me. I used to take my supper from the camp back to my room where Miss Cooper always had plates ready for me and made some splendid cocoa. I felt a bit guilty about all this luxury as I was supposed to "rough it" under canvas so as to get used to rigorous conditions, but I reckoned I had already experienced worse than all this long before everyone else, on the other side of the Channel, and that I would be able to cope with the rigours at any time in the field.

The Army never let one stay in one place for long and without much notice we were moved to Otley in Yorkshire, in the middle of April 1944, and soon afterwards to Bolton-on-Dearne in the East Riding of Yorkshire, as it was then called, and our task was to dismantle Nissen huts on the Irish Sea coast. Faithfully, every morning, three hired coaches would appear at the entrance to our camp and convey us across the country into Lancashire. I suppose they had no "Pioneers" in Lancashire. This was going on for several weeks and made us very late arriving back in camp, due to the long journey. By then our Captain hit on the idea of "piecework", in other words not to work for a certain number of hours, but to go home when we had completed the day's task which he gave us. We had never been back in camp so early and certainly achieved more than we ever did before. Maybe modern industry should try it!

As a result we had a lot of time to ourselves, which was mainly spent in Forces' Clubs, in particular in Doncaster where I fell hopelessly in love with one of the girls looking after us. In fact, I became rather jealous when she devoted more time than I thought she should to other soldiers. She finally invited me to her home, where we discussed the world endlessly until 2 o'clock in the morning, in front of a blazing fire (her father was a local coal merchant). Again this turned out to be another platonic friendship, but for me at least it was wonderful, even if I never slept at night and had to take the first miner's bus back to camp at five in the morning, having wandered around the streets of Doncaster for three hours.

I had meanwhile been to London for interview regarding my application to join the Intelligence Corps. During the interview it was put to me that I should perhaps be dropped into Germany — this was before the invasion — but, as I had not been in Germany since Hitler came to power in 1933, I felt that I was completely unqualified for such dangerous work because of my lack of intimate knowledge of the present circumstances, which is of vital necessity if one is to succeed with such a task. I felt they understood this, but no other offer was made to me at this time.

CHAPTER
EIGHTEEN

It was on June 6th 1944, which later became known as D-Day, when I was just about to give up hope of ever being transferred, that I was suddenly called to the office to see my commanding officer. The order for my transfer had arrived. I was never to see my fellow Pioneers again as I was given three stripes, transferred to the Intelligence Corps and ordered to pack my things and to proceed to London forthwith, where I was to report the following morning!

I felt cheated at not being able to confront at least my sergeant with my newly acquired stripes and to have a meal in the sergeants' mess, but the London train would not wait and transport to the station was waiting for me.

As I had to spend the night somewhere, I had been given a pass to some army outfit, but I thought it would be much nicer to take the train to Farnham and to surprise my mother, which I did by knocking at her door in the middle of the night on June 6th. I do not think my mother even noticed the stripes which I proudly paraded in front of her. All she was interested in was what brought me to London so suddenly and if I had eaten! We talked late into the night and when we had emptied our last mug of "Ovaltine" I became a bit worried about getting to London on time and we started looking at train time-tables. Yes, the five-to-eight will get me there and after questioning the reliability of my mother's alarm clock, which she assured me had never let her oversleep, I went upstairs to a bed much superior to what I was used to.

I had quite a walk to the station next morning and nearly missed my train which I knew from experience always ran on time.

On arrival at my London destination I was given another rail-pass to somewhere in Buckinghamshire.

I came to my new outfit in the Chilterns that same afternoon. Having been assigned my Nissen Hut with a real bed and sheets, I discovered to my great delight that I had been posted to a mixed Sergeants' Mess where good looking A.T.S., Wrens and Aircraftwomen were proliferating, there was even a married couple. This seemed heaven to me, having spent all the war years with men only so far. I was wondering then what kind of people there were and if I would like them better than the Pioneers of 69 Company. I soon realised that I had left parades, reveilles, fatigues and drill behind me and that from now on I would lead a "life of luxury". Our Mess was like a Club, the food was good and plenty of drinks could be bought at the Bar. Nearly all my fellow sergeants were refugees from Nazi Germany or Austria as the job needed perfect German; all had lived in England for years, many had been interned at the beginning of the war, but were gradually allowed to join up. I think I was the only one who had arrived in England just eight months previously in the middle of the war. It was easy to settle in. Our duty timetable was fantastic, 24 hours on and 24 hours off, with the change-over in the afternoon. This allowed us to go to London and spend the night there every other day if we wanted to.

I still remember the beautiful walk to the station, unless one was lucky enough to get a lift. The lovely old-fashioned wooden carriages and the steam engine which pulled the train to Rickmansworth, where electricity took over to get us to Baker Street, stopping at Finchley Road for those who had relatives and friends in Hampstead and Golders Green, where most refugees had settled. Finchley Road, still the longest road in London, was then a tree lined avenue for most of its length and in summer the branches formed a green roof overhead as they do so often in France. I frequently came back at night on the last train from Baker Street.

If one was not going to London, there was a lovely meadow by a river over the Chilterns which was balm to the soul. Later I acquired a bicycle and explored the countryside all around. I felt guilty that I was now able to enjoy life so much when people were dying in the war and for that matter in London day after day.

CHAPTER
NINETEEN

Our duty was to gather military intelligence and any other interesting material from the Prisoners-of-War who arrived immediately after D-Day. My outfit was not concerned with the selection of Prisoners-of-War who were sent to us from the various camps throughout Britain, but it was obvious that most of those who came had been selected for one reason or another, not least because they were good talkers.

We hardly ever got any officers. They were sent to a different camp where they lived in comfortable confinement. From time to time they would have visitors. These would be officers experienced in military intelligence, but some, when they made their visits, would not wear uniforms. Lonely prisoners love to talk and especially to an "English Lord" with a wonderful title. They would open up completely over a glass of beer and in conversation, unhurriedly conducted, reveal all they knew, or certainly a great deal more than they would have done during any interrogation. That the "English Lord" was only a Lord in name did not matter, as long as he behaved according to the German image of a Lord.

There is a word in German which is "gemuetlich" best translated as congenial, and that was the atmosphere which had to be created for all such "conversations".

The most successful interrogators were those who had the patience to listen, but knew exactly what they wanted to find out and how to guide the conversation towards that goal, without appearing too keen. It was normal practice to offer a cigarette and to leave the packet at the end of a conversation and to ask what special requests they had, which would nearly always be fulfilled. This, of course, prepared the ground for the next conversation. It is also important not to make any notes and here is where the Royal Corps of Signals came in. They provided us with what would nowadays be called "the hardware", by installing hidden microphones in all rooms of the compound. An entire building was equipped with listening posts and recording devices, an operation which in later years would become known as "bugging".

It was our job to listen to all conversations amongst the prisoners, who were housed two or three to a room. Often the occupants of the room would have similar voices; as when listening to a radio conversation one could not always make out who was talking; this was of course very important. Even when making sense of a conversation and being able to hear when "A" had finished speaking and "B" started, one still did not always know who had started the conversation, and it was only by listening again and again one got more familiar with the voices and could keep them apart; this was even more difficult when there were three to a room.

All the rooms were numbered and by plugging in our headphones at random into any room, which were arranged just as on a switchboard, we would be able to hear what was being said.

Of course, any interrogation would be recorded if we were advised of it previously. The rest of the time we were roving about to see if we could pick up any interesting conversation having relation to anything of importance in war time.

This task was far from easy and the responsibility was a very heavy one, as it would have been a cardinal sin to miss something which could save the lives of Allied soldiers. Our concentration, especially during the hours of 9a.m. and 6p.m., when most conversations took place, had to be one hundred per cent.

Not only was it necessary to have a complete mastery of the German language, which was not difficult for those of us who originally came from Germany and had fled from the Nazis, but often prisoners coming from regions where dialects are spoken, were extremely difficult to understand, unless one knew the dialect well. In addition, we not only had to be knowledgeable about the whole arsenal of German weapons in all three services — Army, Navy and Luftwaffe, but also know about the ranks of personnel, including the infamous "SS", entirely different from the military. Furthermore we had to be well informed about what was going on militarily and look out for any gossip and information which our High Command wanted to pick up.

We were fed regularly with print-outs of any information picked up by our own unit and by a sister-unit, operating nearby and were then instructed on what subjects further information was required. In order to avoid duplication, so that two people were not listening to the same room, a light on the board indicated that someone was already on to it.

Once a conversation was judged to be of interest or an interrogation was to be recorded, records were cut on a turn-table in front of us — tapes were, of course, still unknown — these were at the normal "78 rpm" speed, then in use for all records. In order to continue recording an on-going conversation, we used two turn-tables as there was, of course, no time to turn a record round. In fact, as soon as we saw a record coming to an end, another one was started, so that there was always some overlapping to prove that nothing had been missed.

Once a record was cut, it would immediately go to another team whose task was transcribing it. This, for me, was the most difficult task, as I could never get everything and I was never one hundred per cent certain that I got it right. I remember how often I was desperate for just one word that I could not hear properly and without which the whole sentence lost its meaning. After back-spacing more than twenty times, thus wasting a lot of valuable minutes, still I often could not make it out. Usually it was an expression which had only just come into the language, or even worse, the name of a place. Often again it was just a question of not being able to hear it properly. The human voice is not always on the same level and many people have a habit of swallowing whole words, if not half sentences. What would I not have given if I could have told them to speak up! Sometimes it was sheer torture, for instance, when outside noises interfered, especially during meal-times — if only they would not have spoken with their mouth full! Even the lighting of a match can interfere.

Of course, it was always a matter of pride, of not being beaten and having to run to a superior and ask him to listen in; on the other hand it was no use to guess, as everything was checked again afterwards for accuracy and one might easily have become the laughing-stock of the Mess, if the guess was wrong or, as it sometimes was, funny. I was always glad when my shift on transcriptions came to an end.

As soon as a second record was cut it would be transcribed, possibly by someone else if the first record had not been finished, and as soon as all transcriptions were checked, they were rushed to the typist pool and then distributed to the various commands, so that they reached whoever should know about its contents without delay. Urgent matters were immediately telephoned through to the services concerned or to the Government Departments interested in them.

In the course of our duties we came across many a horror story. One of the worst I can remember was when we heard from a prisoner that the wife of a camp

Commandant in an extermination camp, had her lampshades made from human skins taken from inmates, selected before they were put to death, because of their attractive tattoos. We had this confirmed more than once! Another time a seaman among the prisoners told how his U-boat captain gave the order not to pick up survivors from an English boat and ordered them to be machine-gunned, whilst they were desperately swimming about in the sea. We also heard gruesome stories from prisoners who had been employed in the extermination camps. There was absolutely no doubt that these were true stories from the people who had actually seen what was going on, as not only would it have been impossible to invent such stories, but the way in which they were told could not leave any doubt as to their truthfulness. Some of the worst reports from the extermination camps which shocked us most, were those which described the callous use made of the victims' bodies after they were gassed.

The military intelligence gathered covered a great many aspects:- We could find out what damage our planes had inflicted on certain targets, sometimes from eye witnesses, at other times from hearsay, and in what way our bombing had impeded the German war-machine and transportation, two of the most important reasons for any bombing, apart from the demoralisation of the enemy country's population. Of course, much of that could be used as well in our propaganda by radio and other means of communication.

The development of new weapons, even the improvement of weapons already in use, the development of scientific instruments, such as radar at sea and in the air, and a multitude of others, constantly came our way, and knowledge of these was of the utmost importance if we wanted to counteract them.

We also wanted to know how effective our newly developed weapons were and whether they inflicted the damage intended. Knowledge of this kind is vital in war-time, as it will shorten the conflict and eventually save lives.

Often potential targets were practically pointed out to us in conversations between prisoners swapping experiences. These were large concentrations of war materials, the manufacturing of essential parts for the war-machine and especially the relocations of important installations after successful Allied bombing.

One day we heard that "Heavy Water" was being produced in Norway and scientists would no doubt have been able to ascertain how near the Germans had come to have an atomic strike capability; it was more than likely that Allied production of the actual atomic weapon was given more and more priority and made progress at a faster rate in view of the reports received from Intelligence, as it would have been a disaster if Germany would have been first to have it.

Then there was Peenemünde, where very secret experiments were taking place. These reports were given top priority, as obviously there was something afoot which looked like a last desperate measure.

Before our bombers started to go over Peenemünde, which was obviously heavily defended from the ground, Intelligence had found out that Peenemünde was producing missiles and soon further information was gathered about mysterious platforms on the French coast.

It did not take long to put two and two together, and when long transporters were observed between Peenemünde and the Calais area, Intelligence knew that soon some sort of bombardment by missiles would ensue. As people who at that time lived between the coast and London will vividly remember, the "V-1" Flying bomb, later followed by the "V-2" rocket, made its first appearance during the night of 13/14th June 1944 and created an awful lot of havoc, especially in London, with great loss of life and property. One could see the "V-1" flying bombs coming over, as they flew quite low and had a flame at the tail-end. As long as one could hear their engines everything was all right, but as soon as the engine stopped it was high time to take cover, as they were then plunging down to earth at an alarming speed with their deadly load of explosives.

Londoners developed their usual stoicism and often watched them with curiosity. However, the damage they caused was horrific, especially when they fell on densely populated areas, or on a large crowded store. At least they could be shot down by our anti-aircraft guns before they reached London, but when the "V-2" rocket first appeared on September 8th 1944, we had no defence against them as they could not be seen or heard before they struck their target. The launching pads were so well hidden and defended and often half underground, that our airforce could not destroy them and the rockets only stopped coming when our invasion forces reached the launching pads.

Another important aspect to watch out for were reports about the morale of the civilian population and those under arms. This feed-back was extremely important for future planning.

Of course not every room could be listened to all the time, and when we just heard the tail-end of a conversation finishing with the sentence "if the British knew that" and not knowing what it was they were talking about, that was really very frustrating; all one could do in such cases was to listen continuously, hoping that the conversation would revert to the subject they might have discussed earlier.

On the whole, it seemed to me that our unit was doing an important and worthwhile job which needed special qualifications. Although I believe that in the Army everyone must do the job to which he or she is assigned to, even if one doubts the necessity of the task, I was glad that in the job assigned to me a positive contribution to the war effort seemed at last believable. As to the prisoners themselves, we never saw them, but of course we knew who the occupants of each room were.

CHAPTER
TWENTY

When armistice came on May 8th 1945, the gathering of military intelligence in Europe was no longer of any importance and most members of my unit were posted overseas to help with the many language difficulties our troops encountered there, especially in Germany itself.

I was getting married in September and I still believe that I was kept back in the U.K. after my fiancée, and now my dear wife Lili, went to see my Commanding Officer, telling him that she needed me here for her wedding! Normally, these small matters were taken care of by allowing compassionate leave for a few days, but somehow she must have been able to convince him that this would not be enough for her. As a result, my posting was cancelled and I remember that I was not too pleased about it, as I was quite looking forward to going and also because I was not too sure what my next assignment would be. For the time being I stayed put, but then, very quickly, new horizons opened up.

In 1945 I was transferred to Wilton Park in Beaconsfield Buckinghamshire, where the Foreign Office had established a kind of University to which specially selected German Prisoners-of-War were sent.

Although Wilton Park was under Army administration, hence the reason for my having been posted there, the purpose of the establishment was not only the confinement of German Prisoners, but to make good use of the time they would still be in Britain.

To this effect a host of civilian German-speaking lecturers from Oxford and Cambridge had been pressed into service. The idea was to re-educate minds poisoned by years of Nazi indoctrination, and to reintroduce them to democracy. The "students" came from Prisoner-of-War camps all over Britain and had, of course, been carefully selected with this aim in mind. Dr. Heinz Koeppler, later to be knighted, was the civilian in charge.

"Wilton Park" was run on the lines of a University. In addition to some 50 lecturers, there were many guest lecturers from public life, among them Members of Parliament, prominent journalists, writers and politicians.

Courses were held on a great many subjects; economical, historical, cultural, political and so on, but the emphasis was, of course, very much on the democratic institutions which we take for granted, especially free speech and the liberty of the individual.

It was a great eye-opener to some of the younger "students" that we in Britain are not only allowed, but even encouraged, to criticise the Government and to put our own ideas forward, as obviously they had never experienced any such freedom in Germany since 1933, when the Nazis came to power.

The themes of the guest lecturers were endless, just to mention a few: "A newspaper in the modern world", "What is my role as a citizen?", "From Weimar to the Third Reich, what has gone wrong?", "How can Germany be re-built?", "Will Germany ever be rehabilitated? And what can be done to help?" The attendance at these guest lectures was not compulsory, but the lecture hall was always full, and observing the "students", one could see how genuinely interested they were.

One of my jobs was to take a number of "students" each week to London and to show them the lies of Dr Goebbels and of Goering, who maintained that all of London was flattened.

This was quite a ceremony, and due to the popularity of these outings we always had a long waiting list. As Prisoners-of-War, their clothes had the usual colour patches on them. Obviously, I could not have taken them to London like that and, in consequence, a whole wardrobe of average size clothing was kept at "Wilton Park" for just that purpose. In the morning of the day a real "dress rehearsal" took place. When everyone in the party was judged to look normal, we set off in an Army vehicle which dropped us at Oxford Circus, where I was left with a bunch of "students" whom I was to bring back again under my own steam in the evening. I am glad to say that I never lost a single one! I feel that the report I gave to Dr Koeppler about the outings can best illustrate why the outings were thought to be an important part of the curriculum:

"We usually alight at Oxford Circus and walk down to the National Gallery via Regent Street, Piccadilly Circus and Leicester Square, where 'students' get an opportunity to see the West End shopping centre and are at the same time introduced into an atmosphere which is, of course, quite strange to them, but to which, judging by their accounts, they get used to very quickly. We stay for roughly one hour in the National Gallery and then walk through Whitehall (where I point out the different Ministries and the Prime Minister's Residence) to the House of Commons. Passing over Westminster Bridge we also get a view of the Houses of Parliament from the river. From there we go to pay a visit to Westminster Abbey. By then it is time for lunch. I like to take Students to the 'Salad Bowl' in Lyon's Coventry Street Corner House where they can eat as much as they like in a nice atmosphere.

It will of course be pointed out to them that not everywhere one can eat as much as one likes and also that one has to queue as a general rule, unless as we do, one comes very late.

After lunch we take a bus to the Law Courts, where we attend a session in the public gallery, this being very instructive. Some explaining will, of course, be necessary. From there we take another bus through Fleet Street, where I point out all big newspaper offices, to London Bridge, from where we get a view of the Tower and Tower Bridge. If time permits we also go down to the Tower, (but not inside, as this is not of great benefit to the 'students'). At 4p.m. we usually attend the service in St Paul's Cathedral after we have

130

had a glance at the Bank of England, the Royal Exchange and Mansion House. The service at St Paul's is with choir and organ music, and the normal ceremonial I believe, is much liked even by people who otherwise do not attend any form of religious service. After the service we have a look at the Cathedral. By then it is dark and if the weather is not too bad we take a bus through the illuminated streets of the West End (a City with all the lights on at night is something not seen by most of the 'students' for a long time), to Marble Arch where we listen to the 'Soap Box' speakers. This is our last activity before having a cup of tea and taking the train back to camp."

Apart from enjoying the outing, the "students" just could not believe their eyes when they saw how much of London was still standing with hardly any damage visible, except around St Paul's, after what they had been told by their leaders! Also the masses of food, including sweets, available at the "Salad Bowl" and the fact that they could come back for more salads and were still not being charged more than half-a-crown, seemed to fascinate them. Of course, 1945 was still a year of severe rationing and even for us the "Salad Bowl" at Lyons Corner House was something special. An amusing thing happened to me after all the prisoners had long gone back to their country and I re-visited the "Salad Bowl" and saw the same girl who used to serve us with sweets (one was not allowed to help oneself with sweets) during our outings. I was then out of uniform and I asked her whether she recognised me and she replied: "Oh yes, you used to come here with them Foreign Buyers"! She was referring to the British Industries Fair which was being held in London every year and which attracted many foreign buyers immediately after the war. I had a good laugh at the thought that my prisoners had been taken for foreign buyers. Perhaps that explains why none of them had ever been challenged when they talked German in the streets.

Back in "Wilton Park" there were other activities as for instance, a printing press, where the "students" printed their own paper called "Die Bruecke" (The Bridge), which served as a future training ground.

It was an in-house journal and also the forum for pieces written by the "students" on a number of subjects and thoughts. Neither the Foreign Office nor the Army interfered with these activities, which were solely undertaken by the Prisoners-of-War themselves and certainly were in line with the whole object of the exercise, which was to let the "students" think for themselves and to get them used to expressing their thoughts in speech and with the pen. It was assumed that a number of them would be future journalists and also work for the media, such as Radio and Television in the new democratic Germany after the war; those going into politics, the civil service and other professions would equally benefit.

I often wondered, having observed this thorough preparation of suitable candidates for what after all would be a new State, why the same method could not equally have been employed by Britain before handing

132

over responsibilities in the many colonies which have gained independence since the end of the war. Maybe some of the newly created States would then have had the benefit of a more enlightened and democratic government.

Epilogue

With so many millions of helpless and innocent victims having perished during the Second World War, I have often wondered why I was one of the lucky ones to survive.

When young, one is not conscious of danger, and life and death situations do not appear to be insurmountable as they seem when one is older. The instinct of survival is paramount.

In my own case, the separation from my family for so many years since leaving Nazi Germany at the age of eighteen, combined with my faith in final victory over evil to which I wanted to contribute, gave me an additional impetus.

My reason for writing this book is my belief, shared with many, that it is the duty of the older generation, if possible, to leave an authentic record of their experiences during World War II for the benefit of future generations. Without it history would simply be hearsay.